THE LIGHT ROOM

THE LIGHT ROOM

Kate Zambreno

Riverhead Books | New York | 2023

RIVERHEAD BOOKS
An imprint of Penguin Random House LLC
penguinrandomhouse.com

Copyright © 2023 by Kate Zambreno

Grateful acknowledgment is made for permission to reprint the poem
"The Uses of Sorrow" by Mary Oliver. Reprinted by the permission of
The Charlotte Sheedy Literary Agency as agent for the author and
Bill Reichblum. Copyright © 2006 by Mary Oliver.

LIBRARY OF CONGRESS CATALOGING-IN-PUBLICATION DATA
Names: Zambreno, Kate, author.
Title: The light room / Kate Zambreno.
Description: New York : Riverhead, 2023.
Identifiers: LCCN 2023000937 (print) | LCCN 2023000938 (ebook) |
ISBN 9780593421062 (hardcover) | ISBN 9780593421086 (ebook)
Subjects: LCGFT: Psychological fiction. | Domestic fiction. | Novels.
Classification: LCC PS3626.A6276 L54 2023 (print) |
LCC PS3626.A6276 (ebook) | DDC 813/.6—dc23/eng/20230113
LC record available at https://lccn.loc.gov/2023000937
LC ebook record available at https://lccn.loc.gov/2023000938

Printed in the United States of America
1st Printing

BOOK DESIGN BY LUCIA BERNARD

For my daughters

CONTENTS

LIGHTBOXES

Otoño

Weeks after the baby is born, summer turns to fall. We begin taking our older daughter to an outdoor class held in an open meadow near the center of Prospect Park called the Nethermead, surrounded by a forest with the park's oldest trees. We meet in a circle dotted with brightly colored plastic blankets, next to a great linden tree that we will see change throughout the seasons, see it green and burnish and molt and green again. Through the following year the children will play at the base of this moss-covered tree, climbing the big knots of its trunk, jumping off again onto the ground. In the distance, under other trees, other groups of children frolic as the adults watch.

The class is conducted mostly in Spanish. The woman who runs it, whom we know, had wanted her daughter to have a parent-child forest school where they speak the language they speak at home, where the outdoors can be its own classroom. She and her family live in our neighborhood, and they have just had another baby, like us—another private pandemic baby who sees faces only at home, as everyone's face out in the world is still covered. We sit together cross-legged on the earth's floor, wearing masks, and nurse our babies. We ask each other how we're feeling; complain about our carriers, which we haven't gotten the hang of again; report on our lack of sleep. We smile at our babies' open faces, marvel each week at their transformation, wonder whether the younger ones resemble their older sisters, our sensitive and intense children, now aggrieved to be displaced as the babies of the family, not sleeping well at night. Her baby, a couple months older than mine, shoves sticks and grass into her mouth, which her mother patiently digs out again. I marvel at her calm, although months later I will be that mother sitting there, encouraging little feet to rub into dirt.

It is difficult to say how I am feeling. I don't have time to think about myself, what with the demands of teaching at home, which started up again only weeks after the baby's birth, and with the demands of the little ones. At first it is a labor walking from the car into the park—through the bridge, past the great trees, the boathouse, up the hill, past the waterfall, into the Nethermead. I carry the baby awkwardly in the carrier, having no muscle memory for it. It hurts my body, carrying her. I go slowly. Everything is slow. After these Tuesday mornings, one of my two days off from teaching during the week, I lie on the couch, nursing the baby all day, my chest tight and painful. Is it from carrying the baby, or holding her on my chest during the day as she sleeps? Am I dehydrated, or not getting enough calories after breastfeeding all day and night? I don't know.

In time the walk to join the group grows easier, although I am still not supposed to pick up my three-year-old, carrying her away from intensities and squirmishes, and I still do, of course I do, how could I not. On these park days I tend not to drink water, as there are still no public bathrooms, and I have to pee the entire time, my abdomen swollen and tender. Although it is uncomfortable to nurse with a full bladder, I peek a breast out from a wool nursing tank top and give it to the baby, sometimes as I'm standing in the middle of the forest, a few paces away from the others. I take my mask off, eager to feel the cool air on my face, to feel some communion with nature. As summer passes into fall, and then into winter, when I get a few weeks off, my body becomes less leaden, grows lighter, I can walk distances without bleeding, and I know then that I am healing.

I worry for my now older daughter, for whom so much has changed, in this year of rapid seismic shifts. Like a meteorologist tracking variations, I watch her, wondering whether she will have an explosion of what I have learned to call "very big feelings," which happens so often at this age, even without the crises of this year. She is set off, on one of the first weeks, when her friend, the daughter of the woman who runs the school, is given a certain toy to play with. The children are all given a bag of supplies, containing a magnifying glass, a shovel, a metal bucket, a wooden spoon, a maraca, a rainbow scarf, each marked neatly in black marker with the child's name. But on this day her friend is handed an additional toy by the teacher. I can't remember now what the toy is, though we hear about it for weeks afterward; all I know is that my daughter grabs it from this child's hand, claiming it was stolen from her. When I try to wrestle it back, she loses control, and I have to carry her—even though I shouldn't—many paces away from the group and try to calm her down. Then she takes off, racing across the field toward her friend, and I feel certain she is going to pummel her, take out all her rage on this unknowing child. When I run after my daughter, which I promise my midwives I am not doing, I carry her away, sobbing like she's lost everything in the world, overcome with mortification and sadness and grief, and still tremendous spiky anger, and we take off early, leaving my partner, John, to pack up with the baby.

Sitting by the lake, we look at the ducks, and I let her eat her cheese and apples, slimy slices sitting in the snack tray her father prepared for her. I hold her and stroke her and tell her how loved she is, that it's going to be okay, and I try to listen. I cry too, because she is sad; we cry together. She doesn't like that every child but her seems to know the language they are speaking, and to know one another. But soon she will be the elder in the group, I reassure her, and she will delight in saying adios to the teachers, and that is exactly what happens. Is this school? she keeps on asking throughout the fall. Am I really in preschool? Kind of, I say.

The next week, she and her friend go to the nearby playground in the park after class and they ride the tire swings together, being swung around by one of their fathers, and all is okay. But then, another time in those early days, her friend and another girl, also their age, take off on scooters, but they don't invite her, and again she breaks down. From that time forward I negotiate each departure so that the three of them leave together, scooting over the bridge, down the big hill, past the ducks, past the weeping willow and the great trees, through the tunnel, before everyone says their goodbyes at the edge of the park, and that becomes part of the rhythm of Tuesday morning. The pleasure I feel seeing their three scooters in a row, a matching candy-colored helmet hanging from each handlebar—grape purple (ours), taxi yellow, a solid green.

By the end of otoño, my daughter is four years old. Her hair is long, and she has grown a full head taller, now the same height as her friends. She takes off fast over the hill, running away from me, laughing, as I call after her. At first it is extremely sunny in the bright open field, and I wear a big straw hat, and we move under the linden tree to sit under the traveling shadow, and then it grows cooler, and darker, and we begin to learn again about fall. I have started to lean into the seasons, their way of measuring time. The teacher, a young woman from Mexico, takes the children on walks across the meadow, has them observe the way the leaves are changing, the linden tree soon covered in yellows and rusts. They walk on the other side of the meadow to the Osage tree, picking up the green spiky fruits that look like textured tennis balls. She tries to get the children to walk with her, as opposed to running away, wrestling and playing, jumping on top of each other, parents encouragingly yelling out to ask consent—Make sure they are okay with that! Make sure they are smiling! An impossible request, when they are all wearing masks, but we manage. Often the teacher will try to get the children to collaborate on some task, moving one of the tree trunks that dot the meadow, or sitting on a large branch and making a seesaw, up and down, up and down. At the foot of the linden tree there is a simple setup for making mud pies. Sometimes the teacher hangs a large rainbow scarf from the linden tree, twisting in the wind. I bring the baby up to it, and she watches the colors unfurl. We sing hello to the babies in the group during the morning song.

Soon we enter the season of rain. The trees are still a lush green, but before long the first dry leaves start to fall. The light is such a specific yellow tilting to brown, here in the forest. We dress our children in Muddy Buddys and rain pants with suspenders, and the boots they are so proud of, whose distinct colors become indistinguishable while stomping in puddles. My older daughter wears a set of sparkly blue, which match the inside blue of her raincoat. As I write this, less than a year later, she has of course already grown out of them. She crouches in her rain gear at the foot of the linden tree and carefully makes mud pies, turning one over and over with her hands, stirring with her spoon, as I hover nearby, observing, trying to encourage her by giving her freedom. She would play with the mud the entire time if they let her. And I could watch her the entire time, and watching feels like a balm I didn't even know I needed. This is what I can give my daughter, now, the ability to get covered head to toe in mud without shame. (Except for her mask, which we try to keep dry and clean.) With my phone I film her dipping a piece of muddy sponge into her metal bowl, and carefully soaking the root of the tree with it. It's so soothing to watch, her total absorption. She loves to splash in the puddles, to get completely soaked, to splash others, to stomp as hard as possible. She loves to sit in a great muddy puddle, which inevitably soaks through her clothes. At the end I rinse off all her rain gear and tools in the water pump nearby, trying not to get muddy myself, as I don't have the proper gear.

The rains that fall are heavier than I remember, at any time, in the decade I've lived here. I know the reason for this, and that it will become worse, and that the sea levels will continue to rise. After a large storm, the pathway through the woods floods and becomes a river that we can't cross except by wading through, and the children, all dressed in masks and rainsuits, splash around in the dirty water, making noises of glee while parents watch at a distance. My daughter is the one in the green-and-brown rainsuit, in the center of everything as usual, bobbing up and down in ecstasy.

Territory of Light

We rent the first floor of an old house that was long ago painted a dark slate blue with now-weathered, once-white detailing and a brick-red front door. We have been here for nearly a decade. Now there are four of us here, plus the dog. We live mostly in the main open room, although there is little that is open about it anymore—tables, chairs, a wall full of bookshelves behind the couch, with more books stacked on the console, where we drop our bags, near where we hang our coats, in a protruding mass that hangs on the side above. My desk sits, cramped in the front window, mostly unused. In the morning, the weak winter light filters through the diaphanous front curtains. Under the window nearest the door the curtain is torn to shreds, from the dog's futile jumping and barking at postal workers and couriers. Often I sit on the couch in this front room to be nearer to this morning light, near also where the children like to play, where we cluster together our chaos.

Each day of the week, one of us teaches at home. A box holding one of our faces or the other, against a background of our dingy room, peering into other boxes of other faces, other rooms. My eyes hurt from being on the computer all day, taking breaks every hour when I hear the baby needs me. "Need," that's the word for the pierce of her hungry cry. When I am teaching or in a student meeting, no matter how we try to arrange the apartment, wherever John secrets himself away with the children, in our bedroom or in my older daughter's room, which used to be my office, I can always hear the baby crying out for me.

Since I began work only a couple weeks after giving birth, at first we position me on the couch to teach my classes, which are now online, bulwarked by pillows, sitting with the towel over a hole our dog has scratched in the cushion, trying our best to arrange the light so that shadows don't fall across my face, in an otherwise shadowy room. Already I feel the weight of overwork on my body, the bleeding into the toilet bowl on days I work too much, which is most days. In November I take on a week-long visiting gig at night, in order to pay for a new couch. Eventually I will sit on this new couch all day, except for the hours I spend teaching at my desk, feeding the baby, trying to get reading or work done on the laptop, or writing notes in my journal as the baby sleeps on me, trying with what little time I have to capture the daily, ephemeral impulse of that fall and winter.

When the couch finally comes, in January, in pieces we have to assemble, it is harder, less comfortable. But it looks more presentable, although generic, for this new life, in which our rooms are the visual background for constant work. Usually kept out of the frame: the blocks and toys and dolls, the filthy rugs, the clean laundry awaiting folding on the edge of the dining table, the packages newly arrived or waiting to be returned, the dog toys, the diaper pail, a baby crying, a dog barking, a child demanding attention.

This semester, I am teaching a graduate seminar on the subject of time. The only space I can find to get any real reading done for the class is in the middle of the night, when I sit up and bear the baby across my lap, waiting for her arm to go limp enough for me to attempt to put her back into the crib. I use the flashlight on my phone to check the thermometer, the radiator hissing and knocking full blast in November, until I wake up most nights sweating through the sheets, and then the radiator failing as we enter the winter. Wake up, take the baby, check the time to see how many hours she has slept, check the thermometer, put her on each breast, hoping she is awake enough to feed, try to pick up the mason jar of water and drink some, replacing my fluids, willing myself not to drop the heavy jar on her head. I give her my breast every time she wakes, every time she cries. The light on my phone throws a shadow against the wall, making me look like a mountain or a ghost. By the end of the semester I am translucent with exhaustion.

In early December, in the middle of the night, with a booklight slung around my neck, I read Yūko Tsushima's I-novel *Territory of Light*, a narrative of a single mother raising her child in 1970s Japan. I am drawn to the pastel shimmery blues and pinks on the cover of the translation. There is a brief period when I am awake, at 4 a.m., or 4:30 a.m., or 5 a.m. every morning, or is it still night, and I move into the other room with the baby, knowing that she needs to nurse, letting her father sleep, and I read the novel, feeling ecstatic in those early hours. At some point, however, the accumulation of sleeplessness causes me to hit a wall, and I am no longer able to read, the exhaustion immobilizes me. Tsushima published the novel in monthly installments in a magazine. It feels like the right time for me to read it now, this work of the vertiginousness of early motherhood, of exhaustion and despair and small joys, of lightness and darkness. I am so drawn to her dreamlike world, which is about stillness and interiority and solitude. I am interested in how the work organizes and contains the seasons, how we move through time.

Although John is at home and helps, more with our oldest, I have never felt more alone than in those early morning hours, in this first year with the baby. I am the one to awake to her cries. I am the one who more easily puts her to sleep. It is with her, and this book, that I begin to meet the night.

The Long Meadow

Every Friday through the fall we head to the other meadow in Prospect Park, the mile stretch of the Long Meadow, to meet up with friends, a boy exactly my daughter's age, with whom she went to a threes class before everything shut down, and his mother. Fridays are mostly my day off, except that I take phone calls with students in the later afternoon, for their conferences and office hours, as I do throughout every day, my breast often in my baby's mouth to keep her calm. Usually I just ask the students how they're doing, about their days, trying to be hopeful or optimistic, at least about their lives and ambitions. My undergrads are trapped in their childhood bedrooms, often miserable in their regression. I tell them to try to go outside. This is a real assignment, as it's a class on nature writing—to be more precise, a class on writing after nature, asking, How do we write amid the grief of climate change? How can we pay attention to both the small and the cosmic? For my part, I still try to find pleasure in a city pastoral, which for me is Prospect Park.

We now get to the park by car, with the baby screaming the entire way, as she hates the car; she is such a joyful baby except in the car, where she feels penned in. In those early months it takes hours to get ready to leave, and we adults often fight, getting out the door, me playing, as always, the sergeant at arms, as I'm always trying to keep us on time. It is inevitably the two of us going there with our two children; we haven't figured out how to delegate, or how to do it solo, but also, despite the frayed edges, we often desire to be together. Plus, everyone expects the mother to show up. The bickering feels constant lately. But we are surviving on almost no sleep while teaching a full slate of classes at various places, with no parental leave.

At first the baby is up every three hours in the night, then every two hours, and at some point it becomes every forty-five minutes or an hour, and by now I've stopped keeping track. There is an element of torture to it. I often send John to the couch to sleep; it's difficult to stir him anyway, to get the baby from the crib and bring her to me, and this way I can more easily bring her back into bed to sleep. The problem is, if I make myself sit up, and check my phone, even start to read, while doing one of these night nursing sessions, the resulting adrenaline makes it impossible for me to fall back to sleep, and even once the baby goes back down, I lie there in the night for hours, eyes closed. No one cares or knows to ask about sleeplessness unless they're going through it. But it becomes clear to us later, how black-and-white our thinking becomes when our sleep is ground down so much, completely deconstructed, how I go to war over petty domestic exchanges, usually to do with getting out the door, while he shuts down. Where is the baby's hat that has the ears, where are her socks, where the fuck are her socks? Why are you grinding coffee again when we haven't found the mittens, no not those mittens, the yellow mittens. We usually say 2 p.m. and by the time we get to the park it is usually three, the baby asleep on me in the carrier. We are always late, in those first few months. We are never not late.

On the first Friday in December, when we go to meet our friend and her son in the Long Meadow, it is gray and slightly raining and peaceful. We pick up coffee and a box of cookies from the Italian place we haven't been to since the shutdown, a treat. By the time we get to the park we are feeling cozy and hopeful; it is always like this, a return to coziness. Usually, after a while, we can't remember what we were bickering about. I drink too much coffee, although I am constantly dehydrated and there are never enough places to pee anymore. The children eat the boxed cookies on a bench, then hand some out to us, delighted in their mission; we take them with our gloved hands, which feels almost too risky, this way of sharing food. Our friend stands some paces away, takes off her mask. We sit on the bench with the kids and accept their offerings.

It feels good, to bring our friend coffee. She is alone all day with her son, as her husband still goes out into the world for work during the day, and even on his days off, he doesn't show. She gets to the park, from where they live, by pushing her child in a stroller for more than a mile. We always see them first, across the field, through the gray drizzly light—her royal-blue knit cap, her son's bright neon yellow. Eventually he will take his scooter there, and she will pull that. She tells me, as usual, about her moms group, as she calls it, now online, and what she's learned about how to communicate with her son, who is prone to tantrums, as is usual still for that age, perhaps even more in this time. She tries this exercise, she tells me again, of picking five minutes to be totally present with him, to do anything he wants. When she tells me this I feel guilty, because even though I am always with my child I almost never get down on the floor with her anymore, preferring to watch from my distance of the couch. Just the day before, my daughter was jumping on the couch while I was nursing the baby, wouldn't stop even though I kept asking her. Finally I swore at her, although I immediately apologized. My friend and I give each other wide berths for our impatience at our children, their tantrums, although I confess to feeling tired of the tantrums of other people's children. Her son's are frequent. He can throw himself on my daughter so totally. Don't go for the face! I've started to call out wearily, half joking.

We had just come from the four-year vaccination. I took her in for the shot, as only one parent could come inside, because of the new precautions. How small she seemed on my lap, without the baby. Her doll got a shot first and a matching Strawberry Short-cake bandage. The doctor, a mother of young children herself, asked me if my daughter was drawing faces yet—a question that surprised me, as she had actually just started drawing faces that week. I still have the drawing on a little table by the couch: an oval body—two arms, two legs, eyebrows, dots for a mouth above a belly button—like a potato person. That's me, she said. The rest of us were blobs, on the bottom of the page, upside down. The yellow highlighter, purple marker, red crayon: these hectic drawings that are somehow beautiful in their chaos.

I tell my friend about this, as we sit on the bench eating cookies. It always feels a little wrong to share milestones, as everyone gets so competitive, especially here. Her son hasn't started drawing faces yet. It'll happen any day now, I tell her, that's what the doctor told me. She doesn't seem to care. She's very no-nonsense, very Maine, if that makes sense. I don't know if we're actually friends. There's a category I think of—the mom friend, whom I see in the park for playdates, whose name I always learn after her child's. We do help each other. When she takes a call for work, we watch her son. We walk across the field to the Picnic House to use the toilets, even though my friend, who has a spry, slim body, often pees in the woods. I won't pee in the woods, as I have a postpartum vagina and I will just pee all over myself, and I'm usually wearing a jumpsuit. When I prepare to go inside, my friend instructs me, in her way, to leave immediately when the toilet flushes. She doubles up her mask to go inside, adding a pointier mask, the first time I've seen one.

Coming out, I see our children attacking each other in the distance. This is not atypical for them, although her son is often the instigator, upset that my daughter's favorite dinosaur is the T. rex too, or that she's standing somewhere he doesn't want her to. The boy is crying now, his mother has picked him up and carried him away; my daughter nearly stabbed him in the eye with a long stick, I believe by accident, and so now I am the one who is apologizing. He's not injured, luckily; only his feelings are wounded. We redirect the children to a large tree, where a school group of some kind has built a fort of branches, common sightings dotting the park this year. They linger there together, drawing patterns in the dirt with their sticks. Such a pleasure, watching the wild children underneath there. They find solidarity after trying to kill each other, John observes. I want them to be able to stand there as long as possible, amid the fort's stark beauty. Instead we all head back across the field together, the yellowing leaves and December light.

Seasons

The day after, we drive to galleries in the city for the first time since the shutdown, a rare outing for John's birthday, wearing masks in the freezing rain. At a show of new work by Etel Adnan, painted during the pandemic, my daughters and I consider her four panels of seasons. The black strokes of trees with dabs of color. Spring is for pink and blue and oranges. Autumn is brown with peach. Is winter the yellowing sky? And summer the swath of pale green?

A woman, who has also been looking attentively at the paintings, comes up to me in that room at the gallery. She is there with another woman, who seems to be her adult daughter. I can't stop looking at your baby, she says. I mumble about how my child responds to the paintings, their elemental use of color and shape, that the baby likes them too. A welcomed interaction in the gallery, but afterward I feel paranoid: Had I exposed myself that way, talking to her inside, though we were both wearing masks? Only afterward do John and I realize that the woman might have been the painter Vija Celmins, a realization in which we take conspiratorial pleasure. It's a relief to be outside the claustrophobia of our apartment, to be together again, seeing art and talking to other people, being in the world.

When we are out in the world, most people now smile at the baby, who smiles back at them. I realize that there's a pleasure, in public, to the open exposed face of a baby. Everyone else's faces are hidden, including my other child's. What I don't tell my friend later is that my child stopped drawing faces soon after she started drawing them. She hasn't drawn faces for some time. I don't know what that means, if anything. I worry whether it's possible that she's stopped drawing faces because she's stopped seeing them.

As I'm writing the above passage, the baby wakes up on my lap. Her pretty red cheeks, like the cherries we saw that day on Cecily Brown's massive canvases. She is becoming sturdier in her body, less fragile. I put my nipple in her mouth so I can continue thinking, folded over. She sucks greedily, falls asleep, moaning ever so faintly. I watch my other one out of the corner of my eye. She is in the holiday pajamas that were a gift from my sister, singing in front of the mirrored closet a passionately butchered "The Hills Are Alive," pressing her fingers against the glass, which won't get wiped off for weeks. My exhaustion today is like a glaze. I have taken to bringing the baby into bed with me at the beginning of the night so I can get a little more sleep, however disrupted. My fingers rest on the back of her neck as she sleeps, to make sure she isn't freezing. The radiator keeps switching off. Our landlord is away and won't do anything about it. I curl around the baby, to give her warmth. I try again to read *Territory of Light*. Once more I begin the opening chapter, reading the same page over and over. Trying to see how Tsushima does it, how she conjures such a sense of lightness as well as melancholy. A mood of cozy dread, that's how I have begun to think of it—I don't know if I read that phrase somewhere. The fiction by Japanese women writers I am reading in translation all resembles this in some way. The alienating chill and slight surreality of capitalism, both in disposable and precarious desk jobs as well as in the hierarchy of the domestic. The longing toward outward markers of success, the hope for transformation if one is promoted to a full-time job or lives in a larger place, a hope that is never realized. And yet there is warmth in the details of preparing food at home, of sitting on a bench in the park, of being with children. The pleasure of the quotidian, of the day, coziness toward one's condition. Maybe that's because, for most of us, that's all we have: the private and the small. The baby is so joyful. Sometimes, at night, I am unsure whether I am sleeping, or reading, or awake.

Happy, happy, my daughter now stomps hard over to her new magnetic blocks in a basket by the front window, separates them, starts building. We shush her. The baby stirs on my lap. Her little foot twitches. She is up, pecking at me. I get her back down. Instead of reading, I watch as my daughter plays with her new blocks, negotiated and paid for by faraway grandparents whom she hasn't seen for more than a year, and who rarely check in. I will wrangle another set from them for Christmas, along with a lightbox, a glowing rectangle of light that she can build on with these translucent blocks. How involved and diligent she is. Building houses from cubes, she then smashes them with a satisfying smack. Smash houses, we call it. I eat a blueberry muffin from the newest batch, and sip cold coffee. My daughter keeps making her boxes, over and over again. At some point she gets bored. I survey the scene. The room is full of baskets I ordered in the fall, in a frenzy of organizing—baskets that fit under the bookcase and my desk, to clear out room for a little block area over by the front window, its translucent IKEA curtains like veils hanging unevenly, cut to size in a hurry. It's so satisfying to me, the wooden rainbow arches my aunt bought her for that first birthday, the baskets of wooden blocks, where the morning light comes in. Where the front room, where we spend all our time, looks the most beautiful. Where I can ignore the dust bunnies everywhere that I must eventually scurry around and pick up, as I must pick up all the clothes and towels on the floor, as I must clear off the main table. All the time spent trying to organize this very small front area, all the baskets I bought, the boxes and boxes of baskets that came in the mail, so the toys could be on the floor or on a low shelf and easier to access. A nesting period. My vision for this year, once I realized I would be homeschooling my child, whatever that means for a three- and then a four-year-old: that if she at least played with blocks, blocks like they'd have at school, maybe she'd be okay.

The novel I am reading begins with a description of an apartment with windows on all sides. All hours of the day, the apartment is filled with light. At the beginning of the narrator's separation from her husband, her daughter is three, as mine was at the beginning of all this, and when they first come to see about renting it, her daughter delights in how beautiful the light is. The woman takes this place, in order to give her daughter this light, to protect her from the crisis of their lives. The narrator describes the many apartment rentals she visited, and the way she documents the layout of her new space conjures up the tone. The way she describes the rooms as boxes, noting details of the small area where she and her daughter would sleep, near an east-facing window, in a storage area fitting two tatami mats, and lingers on the red floor of the kitchen and dining room, that glow where the sun comes in through the windows, makes me feel like I'm entering an installation of light, both the actual light and the buoyant quality of the text, even amid despair. She writes an everyday reality, moving through the seasons, but it is transformed in the writing, in the stillness of the language, the beauty of the gaze. The sensuality and containment of this inside space, overlooking the laundry hanging on clotheslines on top of crowded houses, smaller office buildings, elderly people in bathrobes, taking care of the potted plants they have in lieu of gardens. The view of trains from the bathroom window. The awareness of other spaces, outside and inside, other narratives, not the bubble we are residing in. She narrates a life inside, the daughter missing daycare because of fever, her learning nursery songs to sing to her when she's ill, as they move into cherry blossom season, as they dream of hanging fairy lights out on the rooftop in the summer.

From her window the narrator glimpses a park that she nicknames the Bois de Boulogne. On her one day off, a Sunday, her daughter begs for them to take a stroll in the park. Going outside, into nature, makes her day off more real somehow. Her daughter throws a tantrum once they get there, and her mother slaps her, having reached her utter limit, with the containment and relentlessness of her life, and her daughter runs away. "Why were children the only ones who ever got to melt down?" the narrator wonders, then comes upon a mother she recognizes from daycare pickup sleeping on a bench, another single mom trying to carve out a moment for herself on her only day off, versus the constant maintenance of a child's happiness. The narrator's desire to sleep in on Sundays is also always thwarted, even though she describes allowing the room to become utter chaos as her hungry and bored daughter attempts to pour a bowl of cereal, sloshing milk around, cutting herself when breaking a glass, toys everywhere.

When I read this passage I feel envy for this ability to shut out, even momentarily, the needs of her sensitive, intense child, which I haven't found myself as capable of doing with my own. The narrator also feels envy and wonder watching the mother sleeping on a bench as her child plays near her. She feels a recognition for the other mother that I feel for this mother, this fictional character from the 1970s, who maybe was more like my mother was in the late seventies, having to wrestle three tiny children while her husband was always at work. The narrator imagines a conversation with her, even an eventual playdate, but this solidarity is only imaginary, she never approaches her; when the other mother's apartment building later burns down, due to this same carelessness, she narrates it with the same flat affect. When she finally finds her daughter, after imagining tragedies that must have befallen her, she gives her a horsey ride through the forest; the two share an ecstatic moment as they look up from a weeping willow at the treetops, finding some openness and freedom in nature, together.

I admire how this mother narrator still takes pleasure in being with her daughter, even through the drudgery of constant sickness, through reaching her absolute limit. They are unhappy often, but they also have these moments of being together. I read an interview with Yūko Tsushima, published in 1989 in the *Chicago Tribune*, about how her fictional characters, almost always single mothers, are never happy, but that's because she feels that happy people don't have the required sensitivity. Perhaps, she says, misfortune is not bad. She writes, she says in the interview, as a way to confirm herself, to allow the days to exist in all of their ordinary beauty and awfulness. "If I stop writing, I will feel like a kite without string." There is a specific quality to the ghostliness or disappearance of her mother characters, subservient in their relationships, at work, and as mothers to demanding children. The "I" is present but almost translucent. That's how I've started thinking about these notes I'm keeping, as translucencies.

Early December, the last forest school for the fall. We dress in wools because of the cold. The park is almost completely deserted. The pair of white swans in the lake next to the boathouse remind me of a box the artist Joseph Cornell made in homage to the ballerina Tamara Toumanova, performing in a production of

Swan Lake, the blue glass creating a twilight sensation against a forest scene of trees and houses. Here too in the forest the winter light is bare and still. After coming through the tunnel, my daughter shouting, Echo, echo, while careening past on her scooter, we stop and watch male cardinals in the underbrush, flickers of red. I take a video of my daughter rolling down the hill, over and over, along with her friends, her body covered in brown crumbling leaves. At first the children can't figure out how to roll, so they roll horizontally, giggling. I feel high, again, off their energy. The red wool of her suspendered pants matches the flash of the cardinals, the winterberries in the bushes. It feels like being in another time. I wonder if I am watching myself as a child, brushing brown leaves off my own corduroy pants. I feel so full there, suffused with the circular feeling of the seasons, thinking of the brown leaves of Etel Adnan's fall calendar painting. The only certainty, at least for now, is the changing of the seasons.

In my notebook, I write down a quote from Adnan's *Surge*: "Why do seasons who regularly follow their appointed time, deny their kind of energy to us?"

Fairy Garden

One day in December, attempting to wrestle my daughter down to get her clothes and boots and mask on to go out, to stop her from wriggling, I start telling her a story about a fairy who looks after the stray cats that populate our neighborhood. It is unlike me to tell such a story—I possess little of the romantic imagination parents are supposed to have, especially writers—and she listens, fascinated, as I tug a too-small sock over her foot. I realize, while telling her this, that she is still in this time of believing in magic and fairies. She has a ghost of her own, which she's named after herself. It's something like her shadow. We need to make a fairy garden outside, I say, wouldn't that be fun? I have no idea what a fairy garden is, they weren't part of my childhood, and when she tries excitedly over the phone to tell my father and my aunt, his sister, about the fairy, they don't know how to respond. You see, Grandpa, there's a fairy for the stray cats. I improvise while making plans with her, tugging on her socks. Yes, something sparkling must be in a fairy garden, that's how she's attracted to it. It's a miniature space, a tiny tiny space. Last sock finally tugged on. I get caught up in the reverie with her. Perhaps we can get a little chair, I say, maybe she could paint a rock. In my mind the fairy garden resembles one of Cornell's boxes, where ordinary objects and nostalgic toys—clay pipes and blue marbles and tiny cordial glasses and painted rolling balls—suddenly become kinetic and magic when assembled together. I am probably also thinking of a Tsushima story I had just read in the middle of the night, set in a milieu similar to the novel, except that the narrator has two small children. In this story, the narrator tells of stray kittens abandoned in the woods near her apartment. She wonders who feeds them, musing that the cats perhaps become temporary fathers for the children in the nearby complexes who do so.

For a while, I make promises about this fairy garden. I look up the phrase and discover that it's a whole thing, fairy garden culture, complete with kitschy miniature figurines you can buy. I spend time researching plastic cat figures, eventually buying a little one for my daughter's farmhouse. For the mice, I tell her. Every time I talk about the fairy garden, often when I am trying to get her to be still to put on her winter clothes, she becomes fixated all over again. I can't believe this works. It soothes her, gives her something to focus on. She calls up the cat fairy on the play phone that came with her plastic medical kit. Hello, fairy? Then we make a plan to go to the park, to collect moss and twigs for the fairy garden I find myself promising to make and then putting off. Magic, I tell her, must occur at the edge of the woods.

Of course it's not as romantic as it sounds. That trip to the park is the moment I reach my utter limit, where I break down. John drives us around and around looking for parking. At some point, in response to our inability to find parking, to my daughter's incessant queries or complaints, to the baby's constant unhappiness, to probably some other source of conflict that's been forgotten, I begin screaming as well—screaming to match the baby's screams. My other daughter then joins in, accompanying the chaos, at the pitch they are both capable of. I'm overcome in that moment, the car even more claustrophobic than the apartment. I hear my daughter now screaming in worry as I suddenly get out of the car at a stoplight, and walk away. I walk around the block, the brownstones and tree-lined streets. I know it's cruel to leave when she is so upset, I am supposed to stay and soothe my child, that's what I'm always supposed to do, be the one to soothe the children, with my body, my words, model calmness for them. I feel strangely lightweight, standing there on the sidewalk, like I've escaped. Like I could escape, but where would I even go? I see the car waiting for me on the boulevard outside of the park. They are all waiting for me on the sidewalk. The baby bundled up and now calm on her father, I take my daughter by the hand and go to a bench and comfort her. Sometimes mommies have tantrums too, I tell her, holding her on my lap.

Her father and I don't talk about what's happened. Our silence is a form of forgiveness, or at least moving on. It is always like this, in this first year. We come together, after breaking apart, because what other option do we have? Try to start over each day, hoping someday we can sleep.

We all go together to a spot near the Picnic House, and I manage to dig up some moss with my fingers and put it in a Tupperware container while the child plays. It's freezing, but it's a relief to be outside, to have some depth of field, to stomp around in the mud. It feels like being in something like reality. Later, when my father and aunt call at Christmas, my daughter delights in telling them about this incident, that her mother got out of the car and threatened to leave. I'm DONE, Mommy said, she tells them. Her father and I laugh weakly, the private joke of our bouts of unhappiness, especially since the baby was born, the impasse of this moment, where everything felt impossible. Still, we were hanging on, as best we were able. It was our unhappiness, together, at least, until the happiness again outweighed the unhappiness.

The lump of moss we collected sits in its Tupperware for weeks, until I finally throw it out.

Winter

When the snows came that winter, just before Christmas, I felt somehow that, despite everything, I had managed to give my daughter snow. She hadn't remembered snow like this in her lifetime, the full white of winter, how absolute it was. I wasn't sure that we would have snow like this anymore. My daughter has picture storybooks of the seasons that she flips through, often on the toilet—they portray a cheerful utopian German metropolis. In winter everyone is inside, or ice skating or sledding and drinking hot chocolate, all of which we did that season as well. We went full into the winter season, as again this was something we could do outside, with others. The book is full of subtle meta details I appreciate, like a picture showing a child reading that same winter book in their bedroom.

We had two beautiful snows that winter, storybook snows, and then one blizzard where everything disappeared. The blizzard catches us by surprise. The four-year-old and her father dress up in their parkas and snow gear and go outside to shovel—coming in flushed, happily tired. I stay inside with the baby; I don't have any snow clothes, not even boots that fit, as my feet have widened with each pregnancy. I text my mom friend, whom I'd just seen: Where did you get your boots? She assumes I'm asking about her son's boots. Of course she does. Sorry, it's the mom way, she texts me once she realizes the error—to be sacrificial, she means, to think first of others. For snow, she writes me, she wears track pants she got as a jock in high school. The mourning I feel in my chest from this exchange. I can't really put words to it. The snow brings me back to my childhood, back to my mother and her winter coat, tan, shearling. I always felt reassured by my mother in tough, warm clothes. I'd forgotten what it feels like, to be mothered. I only know, now, mothering. The basket of winter clothes in the closet growing up. Of course I am innately aware of every layer my daughters should wear so their skin doesn't become wet and cold: the merino/silk long underwear, the fleece, the puffers, the gloves, the scarf, the balaclava or hat, the wool socks, the new boots. Yet I have no idea where even my gloves are. I dress my daughter in wool long underwear in ochres and siennas, underneath her rain pants. The chartreuse cardigan that's lasted several years, now short in the arms—this will be its last season for her. I take such pleasure in the layers, in the saturation of colors, her green-and-brown rain pants, her parka, her mask with the planets over her elfin face. Her hair has gotten so long; we haven't yet figured out how to comb it successfully or wash it regularly. Every day we put on all the layers and wrestle them off several times when she comes back inside, too hot, preferring to walk around naked, or at least shirtless, often wearing the red vest of her pirate costume. She walks around changing costumes, with her shirt off. "I'm Marta," she says to her naked self in the mirror. Sometimes, she walks around wearing an old box with holes cut out of it.

Writing this I am reminded of that Mierle Laderman Ukeles series of ninety-five photographs from 1973, *Dressing to Go Out / Undressing to Go In*, showing her helping to put on and take off the winter clothing of her children—photographs mounted on foam board, next to a dust cloth on a chain. Her realization, as an artist with small children, that she should document reproductive labor, maintenance labor, as its own art, because that was the only work that she was doing, the repetitive constant work that disappears as soon as it happens. I saw the Ukeles retrospective at the Queens Museum, our first real outing after the oldest was born. That day I was so out of it that I walked around, pushing the stroller, not realizing until I went to the bathroom that I had chocolate smeared all over my face and the white button-down linen top I was wearing, the only top I had at the time for nursing.

The light of the snow, so blinding that I have to wear sunglasses to see. Later, watching videos of my daughter sledding down the hill, over and over. Again, again. I remember sledding as a kid: The feeling of slush in my sleeve. My cheeks cold and pink. I have been thinking, because it's Christmas, of Joseph Cornell, who was born on Christmas Eve and whose work, for me, has such a winter longing to it—as with his natural history box of butterflies, resembling Christmas windows, splattered with white paint to look frosted. The brightness of his boxes. Robert Mother-well once commented that Cornell's work was "filled with the white light of early morning." The spray-painted twigs and arti-ficial snow as background in his magical *Palace* series, a photo-stat of a grand white or pink hotel, or the silver-painted twigs encasing a doll in one of his earliest boxes from the 1940s, a child lost in a fairy-tale forest. The movement toward brightness in his later series, the white-painted boxes in his *Observatory* variations looking out into dark-blue winter skies and astronomical charts, the empty white cage or room of his Emily Dickinson homage, one blue window; then, later, the dovecote grids, completely painted white, with white balls inside. This is what I saw looking out into all of the white, the brightness of the snow. It trans-formed the open field, so brown and stark, into a landscape made entirely of light.

Walking back to the car on one of those sledding days, past a row of brownstones, many with wreaths on the doors and Christmas trees in the window, I see a profusion of red cardinals in one of the bare trees. Coming closer, I see that the birds are fake, but in the photo I take it's hard to differentiate between these cardinal ornaments, in an outside tree, and the meeting of the red birds in the underbrush some weeks back. It feels like a hallucination, the fake red cardinals in the trees. It makes me feel happy, something so tacky and ordinary transformed into some-thing dreamlike, as in one of Cornell's aviaries, the paper cutout parrots and cockatiels perched in his wooden boxes. I remember now, writing this, that my mother, who loved Christmas, had miniature artificial trees dotted all around the house, in addition to the large real one we'd get every year. One tree was covered with little bird ornaments. Another tree was all miniature copper kitchen utensils, pots and pans. My father still has all the decorations, wrapped in tissue paper and stored in the same boxes. He tries to take them all out every year, or used to.

We've grown used to driving around and around in Park Slope, looking for somewhere to park, then making the trek to Prospect Park, pulling the four-year-old on the sled. The white hills are specked with the bright plastic remnants of broken dollar-store sleds. I've ordered a sturdier sled online, from L.L.Bean, even though the people discarding the dollar sleds probably have a lot more money—the strangeness of discreet and invisible wealth in Brooklyn, where people pay the cost of college tuition for preschools and own brownstones but balk at a decent sled. We pack hot chocolate in thermoses, cut up a large marshmallow into miniature segments, and head off to meet the friends we went ice skating with before. We are extremely underslept again, and because of this we bicker as we walk from the car to the park; mostly because I almost slip, carrying the baby on the ice, the icy path I had asked to avoid. I am also worried she is too cold. The baby is also overtired, past her nap, and I take on her energy, as usual.

When we find my friend, she is wearing the same snow boots as my other friend—like a secret code among people who grew up a certain way. I let the group go on in the distance without me, and sit with the baby on the bench, struggling to get her out of the carrier by myself, in order to nurse her. When I finally manage, and she passes out asleep, I sit back and watch. Prospect Park is transformed into something out of the winter storybook. It is so densely populated across the white landscape, when before, on the muddy brown days, we were the only people here. I listen to people walking by discussing the plot of a new TV show. I see a little brown field mouse scurry across the icy way. There's a story in the Richard Scarry book her father reads to the oldest, that was his as a child—are you a country mouse or a city mouse? My daughter still says this to us: she is a city mouse and sometimes she is a country mouse, like a child version of Madame Bovary. Sitting there, alone on that bench, listening to snippets of sometimes absurd patter, observing the uniformity of everyone's snow boots, I feel that existential floatiness again. Strange to be alone—not really alone, with the baby, but more alone than I'm now used to. These simultaneous feelings lately. I briefly allow myself a spasm of feeling miserable and contained. Allowing myself that self-pity feels close to freedom. But also, how calm I can be, when I can reorganize myself. And look at the baby, I've finally gotten her to sleep, is there anything more gorgeous than a child's sleeping face?

I once read an essay by a writer who didn't want to be a mother because she didn't want to become a landscape, as she would with a baby on her, or so she had read it described elsewhere. She wanted to be a portrait, not a landscape. But the beauty so often of being not a portrait, but a landscape. Of just being part of the landscape. I feel it here too, sitting watching everyone in the park. A collective feeling. The self is a kite sometimes without a string, growing tinier and tinier, until sometimes it vanishes.

Solstice Feeling

In December our sleep deconstructs, even more than before. We are disoriented in our sleeplessness. We had attempted to hold on to the older one's midday nap as long as possible, so we could have a break, even though the baby never sleeps at the same time. But she began to nap later and later in the day, and often she woke up confused. It is dark now at 4 p.m. Is it morning? she would ask. Or is it time for bed? And she would have to sleep again, in a few hours, which never happened. Her father took to lying on the floor at the side, with her squeezing his hand, until finally around midnight she fell asleep, and often now he falls asleep like this, on the floor next to her. By now it is dark all day, as we near the solstice. The absolute pitch of this darkness. Often we forget to have any lights on, trying to protect the baby's sleep.

In the night, when I am up, I begin to see flashes of light. I have wondered at times whether out of the corner of my eye I'm seeing lightning or the moon, or if it's just an ambulance going by. Perhaps I am having mystical visions caused by lack of sleep, like Catherine of Siena. In the daze I'm in, part of me believes this. My body is sore from sleeping on my hip, curled around the baby, who keeps me up, grasping for me. My fingers on the back of her neck, sliding down to her back underneath her pajamas. The heat is going out again in the middle of the night. Now the radiator clamors back on, and soon it is too hot again. The baby strokes my nipple absentmindedly in her sleep. I am her chair that envelops her. We keep opening and closing the windows all day. These city radiators that became a new part of apartment architecture after the Spanish flu, so that people ventilated during the winter, weren't so shut inside with stagnant air.

I spend time when the baby is asleep on me researching the winter solstice. I am feeling so deeply the seasons, their pull and inevitability. I think perhaps this is the way to begin teaching my daughter about time. Every day, I tell her, the earth is slowly revolving around the sun. Tomorrow is the darkest and shortest day of the year, because our spot on the earth will receive the least sunlight because of the tilt of the earth's axis as it spins. My friend texts me that during this year's solstice, for the first time since the Middle Ages, Jupiter and Saturn will reach their closest point in the sky to us. This event is called "the great conjunction." I think of the circle of Etel Adnan's imaginary-planet paintings, like vertical speculative calendars, each circle or half circle including some quotidian element, like a bicycle or a ladder. I take out our planet puzzle, trying to teach my daughter about the planets and constellations. We trace over Leo the lion. I think of Cornell following his favorite constellations. His boxes fascinated with the night skies, rendered in dark blue, often fragments of celestial maps amid a white expanse. A painted cork ball either a moon or a planet, metal rings. A kinetic box for children, but also something that feels so eternal. I look up art projects on the Montessori blogs I scroll through regularly for ideas, including making a Stonehenge with painted marshmallows, until I wonder if I'm losing my mind.

On the day before the solstice, we meet up with our friend and her son at the Long Meadow. The moms sit on the bench with the baby. She's been limping, some mysterious leg ache, possibly from pushing the stroller to get here. They've now been taking the bus, double-masking. How are you? she says. Depressed, I tell her. Yup, she says, incredibly depressed. This is all we can really manage to say; we don't go into detail as to why, because we know why. The constancy and intensity of our children. She tells me she recently started weeping on the phone with her parents; they talked her through it. I say nothing in reply. There's no one in the park, save two older women we always see walking down the path, who smile at us. John is with the kids farther afield, trying to get them interested in their bindles, some fantasy I picked up from a blog, taking linen bags from a cosmetics purchase and tying them to sticks, which they can carry around and use to gather things they find in nature. It amuses me to watch the little ones marching, so tiny and official: Heigh-ho, heigh-ho. It's off to work we go. They get into it for a little while, performing for us, but then they get bored.

The next day, I decide, we will go to the park again and have a solstice ceremony, gathering sticks, acorns, winterberries, to find beauty on that day, to remind us all that light is returning. But when the time comes I'm too depressed to go; instead I spend the day on the couch, nursing the baby. It is so dark and cold. With all this research, I realize, I've been trying to guard myself against despair. And my daughter against despair. Such an intense desire to give her a solstice feeling. To give her light amid the darkness. To remind ourselves the light is returning. Every moment is so full. Every minute exhausting, agonizing, with punctures of joy and beauty.

Constellation (Project for a Christmas Card)

All December I put together what is known as an art cart, filled with art supplies I've been ordering. All these endless boxes arriving. The goal, now that she's not napping, is for the child to be constantly stickering, taping, painting, making play dough monsters with toothpicks and googly eyes and pipe cleaners—playing independently, even though she wants us to watch her. You look like you've robbed a Montessori school, a friend writes me when I text her a picture.

I start setting up play as soon as we wake up, around 6 a.m. On one morning, by ten, I will have watched my daughter glue puff balls and tissue paper to construction paper; play with blocks; have a meltdown over wanting to wear a tie-dye tank top outside, which I hasten to find in a box for summer clothes; become a pirate, a dragon, a magician, a prince or queen; dress up her stuffed bears and elephants. My daughter not feeling loved, feeling lonely, wanting help putting a tiny sock on a doll, miniature doll underwear on a miniature doll. Her long body with its constant vibrations. She kicks the baby. She grabs the dog's paw. I spend so much energy to get her to be gentle toward her baby sister. By the end of the day, my nerves have shredded. I wish sometimes I could just put you in a box, I say to her one of these days. She erupts into tears. I comfort her, console her over her mother's sometime cruelty. How often I lack the patience.

Now, though, she is sitting at my desk, putting neon dot stickers in a sketchbook. I remember this about being a child, the involved pleasure of sitting at my desk with my crayons and markers. From the Montessori blogs, I learn that the way to enlist a child's attention is to issue an invitation. Put the materials on a tray. Arrange them in a pleasing way. Online I find ideas for snow- and solstice-related crafts and art projects: a winter sensory bin made with cotton balls, a special kind of white play dough. I email the links to John over and over, but he ignores them, which frustrates me in my Montessori-induced mania at the time, though now, thinking back, I don't totally blame him. No one needs to be doing this many winter-themed craft projects. Perhaps we can make winter paintings with sparkling Epsom salts. We could make snowflakes out of Q-tips. Or with white pipe cleaners, threading through blue and clear glass pony beads. On a tray I put out a jar of white glue, with a brush, and a white crayon with a piece of blue construction paper. I order up blue construction paper and sparkly snowflake stickers and make her a snowflake tray. She sits at the window and sticks snowflakes on the deep-blue construction paper. A memory, sitting at the table, watching her there: making paper snowflakes with scissors, one of the only arts and crafts I remember from school. Slicing through the snowflakes. The elderly nun, Sister Benedicta—or was it Sister Blanche?—yelling at me.

I watch my daughter at the window, next to our small tree, decorated with felt animals, pink and red paper garland, wire snowflakes, white lights. I think of the Cornell boxes, the way they conjure the feeling of looking through a lighted window. The artist writing in his handwritten diaries, archived online, of the swirl of snow coating Madison Avenue, of the "consciousness of pre-Christmas in [a] quiet way—lights down Main Street through library window." An illumination, an evocation of the past. I have tried so hard—too hard—for the holidays this year for her. The intense sadness and nostalgia of them. The rest of my family has traveled together to be at my father's house near Chicago for the holidays—despite the suggested prohibitions on travel, despite my almost eighty-year-old father's recent recovery from cancer. I feel so alienated from them. I console myself with color. The brown-paper packages, tied with string and red and green washi tape. The blue sparkling sugar for cookies, the blue superhero cape my daughter insists on wearing while making them. Joseph Cornell's love of deep blue and white. On the MoMA website, I see a Christmas card he made for one of the museum's earliest directors, who exhibited Cornell's boxes: a background of paper painted deep blue, with white gouache over it, and the impression of a small bird. Inside, a poem and inset small collage of the bird, with a metallic blue star sticker. *Constellation (Project for a Christmas card)*. When the baby naps on me, her father takes the kid and the dog out for rambles—I'm going exploring, she says. She carefully trains the binoculars her grandfather has given her for Christmas up to the blue jays screeching in the trees. When we tell my father this over the phone, he is thrilled. How nostalgic he is for anything that resembles his childhood.

Over Christmas I am in bed with the baby, making little notes about Cornell, trying to feel better about my despair. His biographer wonders how he dealt with such a cloistered life. The supposed misery of living with a brother in a wheelchair and an overbearing mother. The assumption is always that he was miserable. "How could he have made it under the circumstances in which he has?" Robert Motherwell wrote. I wonder why a small life is always read as a terrible life. My domestic life is also ordinary and chaotic. Trapped inside this apartment, sometimes, it is cozy, even if at other times it is miserable. Perhaps I am a writer of the interior, I write to my friend Sofia on Christmas Eve, of circumscribed walks outdoors. I've always been like this, though the feeling is made more pronounced because of the pandemic and the second baby. I'm glad not to be traveling, not to be socializing, not to have playdates this week, not to see family. I wouldn't be doing that anyway. I would be in bed with a baby with milky coffee, reading this Cornell biography and taking notes. I would be taking walks in the park with John and the girls and the dog. Of course you may well travel again, Sofia writes me back. But perhaps interiors and circumscribed walks are the elements that compose your soul.

At twilight yesterday we took a moonlight walk. Just like *Harold and the Purple Crayon*. We followed the moon and saw the fairy lights in the windows. My child insisted on wearing her robot costume as we walked around the neighborhood, a metallic box slipped over her head, which her father helped make, and I remember now the shine of the tinfoil in the moonlight.

Flashes

I keep seeing the flashes of light in the middle of the night, when I sit up after nursing to check the temperature or the time. I worry it's related to the high blood pressure I had after the baby was born. Or perhaps dehydration—I'm always dehydrated, especially in the night, when sitting up to drink water increasingly feels impossible. Is it like tinsel? someone replies to a post entitled "Seeing Stars," on an online breastfeeding forum from years ago. Exactly! Like tiny pieces of tinsel floating around. The baby sleeps on my body, making gurgles and spits.

It is my birthday in two days, at the end of December. I am dreading it. All our birthdays fall within a month of one another, except the baby's. There is a birthday banner hanging at the window, made of rainbow-colored felt, and we keep it there because it cheers us. It's homemade, though not by me.

In the morning I am immovable. The constant dehydrated feeling, like a hangover, from the night. My entire body aches. Sore feet. Unwashed face all day, no moisturizer. My hair's been falling out. I've been sleeping in for an hour or so, letting John take the morning shift. He hands me waffles and turkey bacon while balancing the baby on his hip. With her pretty face she studies our faces, trying to figure us out. Then gives us the most joyous grin when we smile at her. Although we so often delight in her, sometimes it's devastating to realize we are the only faces she sees. The dog sits at my feet and licks his lips, his paw on the bedsheets. Bananas in the waffles today. My daughter is in the other room belting a Daniel Tiger song. Her father gives the baby a kiss, moves her higher on his hip, tells me about the hour I missed. Big exercise session, he says. She's turning the page now when we read. They took out the garbage together, waved at the maintenance worker. We are trying to keep things light again. I try to acknowledge the times he takes care of me, as I take care of the others. Sometimes we are frazzled allies, other times the devastation. Often on the same day. It depends on sleep, and on how much he has been able to help the night before. We keep track of sleep, count the hours, each convinced the other had more. The one with more sleep owes the other. In those early months, I am never the one with more sleep.

I often lie there an hour or so, unable to get back to sleep, hearing screams in the other room. Screams of play, screams of frustration, screams of pain, screams of needing Mama. From both girls. The sound erodes me. The less I have to speak in the morning when I wake up, the more I can at least turn language around in my head. The baby cries, and I take her back. I cover her in kisses after nursing her. Her father is reading to her sister in the next room. My waffle and coffee are now cold, which usually happens. Finally, the four-year-old comes in and asks me, in a beseeching tone, to play with her. I bring the baby out into the main room where we spend all our time. Detritus from yesterday's play still everywhere. I will myself not to focus on it. My daughter turns on her new lightbox. It glows in the corner of the room. She builds a cube of magnetic blocks on top of it and it glows blue and red and green. Later I will put out her new translucent mosaic tiles for her, stored in a clear case I took pains to get. Six components, six shapes and colors. Later she can transfer, organize, count. I watch her at her glowing rainbow box. Watch the white lights on the miniature tree. The baby plays with a fabric puzzle ball with her feet. I'm making the future, the oldest says in a fake British accent she has somehow learned from cartoons.

By noon my nerves are already frayed. The baby is teething and overtired. I focus my entire body on soothing her. Her face red. Her little feet rubbing against each other for comfort. I give her the nipple until she takes it. Roll her on her tummy, roll her on her back. This is how we measure time now: a tooth, its first suggestion as a red swell, until it finally cuts through, emerges. The world: a tooth. John comes into the room to help. She is my focus, until finally she is knocked out, asleep. Her sister is nearby, dancing around naked, making up a song. How long her body has become. It surprises me. We've been inside all this time, and she keeps on growing. With the baby heavy and comfortable on my lap, I spend time brushing out the large knot in my daughter's hair. I let her gnaw on the remnants of her chocolate Santa while I do this. As always she is shirtless—that hair down her back she refuses to let us wash, or you're going to get bugs, I tell her weakly. I think of Natalia Ginzburg's essay "Winter in the

Abruzzi," about her Jewish family living in the Italian country-side for three years under Fascist rule, of her dressmaker dividing the young women there into two types: those who combed their hair and those who didn't. Those who didn't got lice. The dressmaker recommended a young serving woman, who did comb her hair, for the family—not a woman, Ginzburg notes, but a girl of fourteen, who told the children fairy tales of death. When Ginzburg first arrived there with her family, she writes, she couldn't distinguish old from young—the women there lost their teeth at thirty, from too much overwork and breastfeeding, having so many babies in swift succession.

Abruzzi Feeling

"There are only two seasons in the Abruzzi," Ginzburg writes: "summer and winter." By winter, the shoeless children had disappeared from the streets. Everyone stayed inside, cooped up in their dingy rooms. Winter in Abruzzi was about a series of interiors, "enormous, gloomy kitchens with hams hanging up, and huge, empty, squalid rooms." You could tell the rich from the poor by the quality of their fires. It was when the snows began to fall that the narrator's sense of exile became real; shut away from their friends in the city, the children forgot what their life there was like. Though their homesickness sometimes had a pleasant quality, after too much time inside it turned sharp, bittersweet, something like hate.

Our families have never met the baby. It is only us; we have no help. In those early months we fight over housework, over homeschooling. We each just want some time alone. But where would we go? In these weeks off from teaching I go into a frenzy, making lists of chores to do around the apartment: replacing the broken fridge drawers, ordering more baskets, more trays, sealing the window so it's not so freezing in the bedroom. John worries over the smell of leaking gas in the foyer. The temperature is in the sixties, then goes up to the eighties. When the heat goes off, we take hot baths. He always makes a hot bath for me, but eventually children get added in. I sit in a bath of my own worry and, eventually, naked children.

Ginzburg's family also did all their living in that one room. That is where they ate. The husband, whom the people in the countryside took to calling "the professor," wrote at a long table. The children's toys scattered around the floor. So much of the scene she conjures feels like the Christmas we are spending here: He prepares food in the kitchen. I sit in the main room, the big room where we do all our living, and watch the children. The four-year-old comes into the room, her beautiful pale body naked under her open red robe, reciting lines from *The Sound of Music*. She always forgets the names of the girls and I have to remind her. "Who am I?" she asks. Liesl, I tell her. "Oh yes," she says. "I'm sixteen years old and I don't need a governess." She doesn't care if the baby is asleep. If we shush her too much or tell her to get down from the furniture, she will begin to scream, a high-pitched shriek. Her father will then come out and issue a series of comically hyperbolic warnings: if you keep climbing on that chair, you are going to fall and your head is going to smash and it's going to bleed everywhere. I play referee. Sometimes it is all so claustrophobic that I start to feel translucent, completely worn down—what I think of as an Abruzzi feeling. For comfort, I watch the construction and collapse of cubes of light: how they glow, like an installation. Red squares beaming purple on top, thanks to light from the blue floor below.

To escape, the family in Abruzzi took daily walks in the cold and snow, shocking their neighbors. Babies born in the winter were meant to stay inside until summer, the only other season. At the end of December we keep up our weekly trips to the Long Meadow, now alone, as our friends are visiting family. It is freezing outside, a relief from our often overheated apartment. We look up at the birds in the rich blue sky, the white clouds. My daughter and her father try to fly a kite, but there's never enough wind. We try to guess the numbers once represented by the collapsed foil balloons in the trees, casualties of park birthdays. How many birthdays will my daughters have, living here, like this?

Ginzburg wrote "Winter in the Abruzzi" in Rome in 1944, after they returned to the city and her husband was imprisoned and executed for resisting Fascism. Near the end of the essay, she describes the philosophy she learned through her family's three-year confinement in their small village, and through the anguish and horror of her husband's solitary death in prison. "There is a kind of uniform monotony in the fate of man," she writes. "Our lives unfold according to ancient, unchangeable laws, according to an invariable and ancient rhythm. Our dreams are never realized and as soon as we see them betrayed we realize that the intensest joys of our life have nothing to do with reality. No sooner do we see them betrayed than we are consumed with regret for the time when they glowed within us. And in this succession of hopes and regrets our life slips by." Only now, she writes, does she realize that those days of buying oranges and going for walks in the snow were the happiest days of her life. But when she was living in exile, she always looked toward another, more hopeful future, where her dreams and goals would be realized. She ends in an elegy—to her husband, but also to the impermanence and ephemerality of time, of the slow certainty of everyday domesticity, of a time when she thought she was miserable, but later realized that within that misery glowed something like joy.

Birthday

I sit and drink milky coffee on the couch while reading the opening of *Family Lexicon*, Ginzburg's memoir of her childhood. While trying to read, I watch my child build on her lightbox in the corner of the room, near the window. A city, she calls it. I worry over the rash on the baby's neck. It is my birthday. I am forty-three years old. Doesn't seem fair, for birthdays to count this year. I read the preface again, written with Ginzburg's characteristic drollness. No names are changed, she writes. They are the real names of real people. "Perhaps someone will be unhappy to find themselves so, with his or her first and last name in a book. To this I have nothing to say." But still, she writes, it should be read as a novel. There are other things she does remember, she adds, but chose not to write about. "I had little desire to talk about myself. This is not in fact my story but rather, even with gaps and lacunae, the story of my family."

I find myself lingering on this preface, which is also a statement about writing the self. Perhaps it is not about facts of the self, but about finding something else. Something of how family exists together, in the light of day. That's a Ginzburg formulation I read in an essay she wrote on her friend Italo Calvino: that his earlier work has the beauty of the light of day, but *Invisible Cities* contains another light, a more inward light. "Gradually, the vibrant green landscapes, the glittering snow, the great light of day disappeared from his books. There emerged in his writing a different light, no longer radiant but white, not cold but utterly deserted." I wonder if this is what I'm doing now, with this winter notebook. Trying to find the beauty of the light of day, the dazzling snow, the texture of the landscape. Trying to find beauty in the ephemera and fragmentation of the memories of these years, of being home with my children. Attempting to write something of the specific winter light. To reflect life like a piece of photosensitive paper, Sofia suggests.

Even though I am now one year older, there is still the case of the baby having a rash. She sits there on the floor, spinning with one hand her little wooden rainbow drum, the mirror flashing and marble rattling around and around. The baby joyous with a rash on her neck. She needs to be stripped, cooled down, because it is boiling in the apartment, the radiator wheezing; she has had a cool washcloth applied to said neck, has been put in a comfortable cotton onesie for her nap, the other two hurrying out, getting dressed in various corners of the apartment, usually right in front of me in the same room, in order to go to the local library, which is finally open for outside pickups.

Later in the day I bring *Family Lexicon* into the bathtub. Today I am allowed the luxury of a book, of a bath. We always pretend at first it's going to be my bath alone. Ginzburg narrates being homeschooled by her mother for the first few years of her education. The character of the overbearing scientist father. The parallels to now, to my homeschooling my daughter this year, if that's what I'm doing. "I didn't go to school even though I was old enough because my father said at school one catches germs." The mother in *Family Lexicon*, reading the paper all day on the couch—I wonder if that's what I'm like, if that's how my daughters will actually remember me. A funny passage about the mother who teaches mathematics with candy and beans, who envies a friend who knows the names of plants when they take nature walks. My desire to learn how to garden, maybe grow herbs in the kitchen. And yet I don't. Maybe I'm lazy too. "I am a scientist," my daughter says. "Because I'm curious."

The baby is cranky so I let her come into the bathtub to nurse once the water cools down enough. I caress her little red wrinkly rump, the rolls on her thighs. It's still probably too hot. My other one then approaches and asks if she can come in. Previously she had been running around, alternately talking in a secret language and reciting Charlie Brown monologues, playing a game with a chewed-up dog ball and a Popsicle stick. She strips off her pirate's vest and gets in, giving her sister a kiss and nuzzle—this week she has decided she loves her, her baby sister who chortles loudly at the sight of her face, at her antics, who gives her more than the mirror and her parents to perform in front of. Her father now is doing a video call in the bedroom with the pediatrician about the baby's rash. Her sister lies against me, we compare our feet to each other's. I massage her face. She is excited that it's my birthday and she gets to blow out the candles on the cake her father is making. She splashes me. I splash her back, which surprises her. "Mommy, don't be an asshole." She has started to call people assholes because I do.

When Natalia Ginzburg recalls those brief intense years of having little children, whether her own or her childhood reimagined through her mother's gaze, the memories are always sepia-toned with nostalgia, though spiked with a wariness and wit. Ultimately the memory of the chaos is a happy one. "And later, really the years when she still had all her children at home and there wasn't any money, and the price of the property shares were always going down, and the apartment was damp and dark, she always spoke of that time as beautiful and very happy." The baby's smile, even at 4 a.m., is so radiant. The baby no one has seen. We are the only faces the baby sees. Her smile so gorgeous and bright. How she stares at her sister and at us. Sparkle face, we call it. Sometimes I will roll over, having dragged her into bed at some point in the night, and see her smiling face. Oh, sparkle face! Sparkle face! Please sleep!

Clearings

I remember that January as stomping around in the field, the strange, almost spooky gray light cutting through, the different textures of the winter mud caking our boots, in order to somehow shake myself out of the depression that had overtaken me, even more than before. Sometimes the sky had clouds like putty, other times it was unimaginably clear, tinted blue, with an almost overbearing noon sun. We are completely alone on these mud days— in the blizzards, bodies filled the park. A long walk in Fort Greene Park for New Year's with our friends. All of us have sniffles because of the cold. Still, to look at the stripped trunk of a maple or oak is happiness. To be all together outside is happiness. Standing in the mud surveying the distance is some of the most alive and present I have ever felt. I realize I go mud-stomping in order to try to feel something—some feeling of elation or ecstasy. That somehow I was able to feel this, this relief of being outside, released from the relentless rituals of the day. The children are splashing around in the deep muddy puddle that has formed in the path. The river, they call it.

In his diaries, which I finally get from the library, Joseph Cornell writes often of "clearings," which I take to mean moments when he could finally think, or see, have some space inside his head, but that were also linked to his minute documentation of the weather. These clearings often had to do with his "cellar work," the work he did in his studio that he made for himself in the basement of his mother's house, which was both for archiving primary materials, all of the sources for his variations, and for the actual construction of his boxes. Upstairs, the crowding of the domestic; later, when both his brother and his mother had died, reminders of his grief. Often, through the cellar window, he would watch the birds during the winter; when it was warm he would sit on a chair in the backyard.

In one entry, the gist of which repeats often, he writes of "gratitude for the 'clearings' during day." Often he would record light: whether the sun was out, the reflection of the sun on the cellar window, often through the foliage, when it was bleak outside in the winter and there was no sun. He would record the constellations he saw and how clear the night was—the "clear frigid splendor" of seeing Orion one December night. He would record not only the physical light, but also an "illumination"—a word that repeats throughout the diaries—that occurred, due to some "sparking," of the elements, or a memory, or a sighting, a stirring of nostalgia, an evocation of the past. He wrote often of his feelings: dream feeling, transcendent feeling, unexpected feeling, nervous feeling, unexpectedly elated feeling.

His goal with these "pennings," or "scribbles," as he called his diary practice, was to document something of the ephemeral, of the everyday, to reach toward this feeling of illumination or revelation. He often worried about why he wrote so often in his diary, notes he habitually made on scrap paper, envelopes, leaves of a tree, pamphlets, and transcribed sometimes only years later, like the fragments of his beloved Emily Dickinson. On a January day in 1960 he wishes to "extract from the scribble something sublime and sunny." In another entry, he worries over why he is attempting to keep this diary at all: "mistake of trying to catch something sublime—vital—and digressions into personal diary of present—many related experiences . . . wonderful & beautiful but what are words! & all those notes?"

I too don't know why I need to write everything down. I have no time or space to keep a notebook anymore, so I write fragments and scraps, sometimes incomprehensible. I think that's the desire—with digressions, with the day, to catch something that's vital or sublime. But all I have is a vast archive of notes, so many of which are variations, repetitions. Joseph Cornell's fear of the day getting lost without his diaries, the "necessity and difficulty of capturing experience 'before it fades.'" As I read the diaries from the couch, I watch our daughter put wooden peg people into her rainbow house. It is now a massive castle. I sit there and watch the filter of rainbow light through the window, like stained glass. John plays with the baby in the other room. I sip my coffee, balancing my notebook on the nursing cushion, enjoying my little dog resting at my feet, my constant couch companion, perched on a pillow covered in a green striped wool blanket. On the evening of July 16, 1963, Cornell writes of a "couch dream." A "great sense of everything white—but more than just physical ambiance—a sense of illumination." Is this what these paragraphs are? Are they lightboxes?

Lighted Owl I

This paragraph is a box, containing the soft winter light of that January landscape. Another exhausted Friday playdate in the park after teaching all week, as the semester has resumed. Eyes wearied from the artificial light. In a state of almost mute retreat. My time is not my own again. I have lost that occasional space of contemplation of the break, giving myself over to others, their feelings and narratives. Still, on our days off we retreat to the park. I am on a bench nursing the baby, bundled up in brown wool bunting. A photo from that day shows us squinting together, her chubby pink cheek against mine, my absurdly high gray wool hat matching hers. In the distance the two children pick up sticks, mostly companionable, with occasional spikes of aggression, as my partner follows after them. On the bench, I watch them go up and down the hill, looking for dinosaur tracks. Later, when we are walking together, the boy asks me why there are valleys. They were sculpted by glaciers, I tell him, although I don't really know. But it turns out, when I look it up later, that I was right—that the long unbroken meadow was formed seventeen thousand years ago by a glacier. The children carry huge sticks; we tell them to keep them pointed low. Two other humans in this preapocalyptic landscape. An elderly man with a cane walks around with a metal detector under one of the trees. I allow him, his eccentricity, in our solitude, but not the asshole scaring a circling hawk with a drone. Only us, usually, and the valiant daily walkers, and the birders, and then this asshole I cannot categorize. As usual my eyes take in the sandy browns and textures. The brown curling leaves everywhere. The coldness and brownness. The mud squeaking underfoot. A pressing yet gloomy light like a secret. The austere sculpture of the trees. I study their gnarled roots and branches. The surprise of the green moss. How gorgeous the devastation of this terrain.

All this reminds me of the diorama-like settings of Joseph Cornell's owl boxes, which he constructed in the 1940s and '50s. On bicycle rides through the suburban countryside, once he had moved into his family's house on Utopia Parkway in Queens, he would collect moss, twigs, bark, and dried grasses that he would then put through a powdering or pounding process in his cellar, like an herbalist in an apothecary. The physicality that went into working on these owl boxes was part of the joy for him. The bicycling, the gathering, the breaking down of the materials in the cellar. Also the labor of making their habitats, the wooden boxes. He worked on the owls at night, the cellar another nest to make his "deep forest interiors" and "woodland habitats." In a diary entry he records "the many trips made by bicycle gathering dried grasses of different kinds, the fantastic aspect of arriving home almost hidden on the vehicle by the loads piled high/ the transcendent experiences of threshing in the cellar, stripping the stalks onto newspapers, the sifting of the dried seeds then the pulverizing by hand and storing in boxes. These final siftings were used for habitat (imaginative) boxes of birds, principally owls. The boxes were given a coating of glue on the insides then the grass dust thrown in and shaken around until all the sides had an even coating to give them the aspect of a tree-trunk or nest interior." As in his other boxes, Cornell is also collecting something from the past, some memory of childhood that yearns toward transcendence (even as the absorption in the work was its own form of transcendence). The nostalgic feeling of being out in the rural meadows and among the old houses, which might have reminded him of his more rarefied childhood in the family's Victorian house in Nyack, when his father was still alive and the family was intact and prosperous, of vacations in the country.

Lighted Owl II

After saying goodbye to our friends, we wander off and find ourselves in an area of the park that we've never explored before, a play area set off by a group of fallen trees. The stumps of the trees in a light that's somehow both spooky and sharp at the same time—the pale ears of mushrooms still growing within the logs, long after they've been cut down. In a diary entry in late summer 1946, Cornell records bicycling in the afternoon and coming upon a gathering of stumps in a cleared field, upon which he located several pieces of fungi that he would later use for the owl boxes. I have a photograph of my oldest from that day at the playground of fallen trees, standing in the middle of a rect-angular tunnel, like a door, cut out of one tree. She holds a stick with her mask at her chin, as I had asked her to pull it down for the photo, and she is wearing her black coat, putty-colored rain pants, mud boots, her dirty curls down her shoulders. How tough and yet contemplative she looks. Her black puffer is getting too tight; she won't wear it another winter. A photograph of a child is already an elegy. That was almost a year ago. How is that pos-sible? I don't understand anymore the texture of time. Is it solid or permeable?

A photograph is like a box. There is a box, as a frame. The door, another frame. We go inside a window. Nestled inside my care-ful and constant frame, my daughters are little owls, their faces still like moonlight within the forest sanctuary. The paper cutout of an owl, yellow plastic eyes pasted onto a flat piece of wood, like a ghost silhouette amid a field of bark. The contrast of the artificial and the natural, like the dimensions of a natural history museum diorama. The blue-tinted glass and interior electric lights of another of Cornell's lighted owl boxes, which gives the ap-pearance of a shimmering curtain of moonlight, a sense of depth as in early photography, the owl nestled on a bough amid a forest interior. In his diary the artist recorded visions and sightings of illumination, a description that resembles the effect of his owl boxes. Sometimes these memories are of another season. In Au-gust 1947 he writes: "Moonlight in kitchen illuminating objects with an ineffable softness—enhanced by being reflected from snow."

I have another photograph on my phone from that early January playdate. The children with their bike helmets on the immense mound of pitch-black dirt they call Dirt Mountain. They climb up this hill, roll down it again. As if they are the last people on a scorched earth. That day I had brought them a plastic baggie full of nubs of pastel chalk and they had taken turns scratching on an enormous tree stump nearby. I showed them the moss growing there, reminding them that there is still life here, a vast network. The photograph shows the two children in that moody light, making themselves a maze out of the tree stumps. I can't see it in the photograph, but I know they've been hard to catch still, they're running around, exploring.

Days later, we went back to the newly discovered playground of fallen trees, for a playdate with the children and parents from the Tuesday forest school, during the session's break for winter. The baby was cutting her second tooth, her central incisors, her red cheeks and face damp with drool; we let her bite our fingers even though it was so sharp. Lately she has taken to crying like a cat. Two teeth that January. A tooth has become for us a unit of time, more than a day, sometimes weeks, waiting for the eruption. All these cycles, ways to measure time—seasons, when we last saw friends, stages of tooth eruption and hence sleeplessness. The three friends from forest school scooted up and down the sandy hill, with such speed and force, eventually ripping off winter coats, hats, too hot, masks wet from sucking on them, in love with speed and their bodies. Parents stood around watching their children with a studied squint, talking about vaccine bureaucracy, teaching over Zoom, speculations about if and when this all will end. I watch the birds overhead—are they migrating?

The three girls found a fallen tree to use as a balance beam, asking their parents to help them jump down from its height once they got to the end. They picked up a large, heavy stump together and conspired to carry it to the entrance of the hollowed-out tree, the adults laughing in the distance. Firewood, they said. The three of them stood inside the hollowed-out tree. We laid the two babies on the ground next to each other in their bunting. They smiled. Their sisters patted their bellies like drums. Many months later, in another season, I come upon this same hollowed-out tree. I had forgotten something I'd seen inside it: an illustrated poster, the famous image of George Floyd. The poster has since been painted over with blue. There is blue painted graffiti as well. I don't stop to read it. How apocalyptic and unstable everything felt, that early January. The encroachment of fascism. But still we watched our children play.

Lately I have been thinking about Italo Calvino's lecture on lightness, which he wrote for a series at Harvard in the fall of 1985 but never gave, as he died of a cerebral hemorrhage before leaving Italy. The lectures are about his values for literature in the coming millennium. He finished all but the last of these six memos. All that is known of the last is that it was supposed to be about consistency. He was only sixty-two. He had planned to write fourteen more books. Usually when he wrote, he said in his lecture on lightness, he attempted to remove weight. Sometimes

the weight he subtracted was from cities, sometimes from constellations, sometimes from language and plot. Perhaps it was
really the facts of his life, the weight he attempted to remove, or
perhaps it was the opacity and inertia of the world. "At certain
moments I felt that the entire world was turning into stone."

The last time we saw our other friends, our Friday friends, that
winter was sometime that January, on a trip to the Prospect Park
Zoo. The husband had gone into quarantine in their bedroom just
hours before, because of a positive test at his work. We still went
with them to the zoo, we didn't want to cancel a Friday, to aban-
don her. She was on the phone for most of the afternoon, ordering
an air purifier, making plans, a little frantic. At the farm I put
quarters in the feed machine for the children, twisted it for them,
poured the pellets into their hands. Gave them more quarters at
the ducks and turtles. In front of the sea lions, at the sculpture
of the lioness and her cubs, they played on a frozen mound of snow,
the last remnant from a month ago. At one point the boy was
on the verge of a meltdown, and I pointed to a tree with a large
hole in it to distract him. What do you think sleeps here at night,
I asked him, an owl? The children stopped and looked up.

We had just been to the larger zoo in the Bronx, the cages of
the white snowy owls and barn owls perched on a profusion of
branches and underbrush. Both a natural and an artificial environment, like dioramas and Cornell's natural history boxes. In
one of his lighted owl boxes he placed small pieces of dried dyed
lichen, a rubber lizard and rubber spider attached to dried wood.
Around this time a snowy owl was spotted in Central Park, the

first time in over a century. In the sand of a baseball field. The outside dance classes I took my daughter to that month, on the baseball field in the Parade Ground—girls in parkas, all neighborhood friends, digging with sticks in the sand. But soon those classes stopped as well. Soon we stopped doing anything. Another blizzard came. Then another variant. We spent the month of February inside.

It was around this time that my daughter stopped sleeping. We had decided it was time for her to give up her pacifier once and for all, because even after dropping her nap she wouldn't go to bed until 11 p.m. or midnight, and then would wake up in the night. A belt in the dark: Daddy! Mommy! She wakes us up, which wakes the baby up—or sometimes I'm already up, since the baby has woken me up, and I'm sleeping on my side on my sore hip, attempting to go back to sleep, my mouth also sore, as the dog had chewed up my mouth guard one day while we were at the park. The radiator rattling on in the night, the temperature sometimes reaching 80 degrees in her room. One night she wakes up having wet the bed, unusual for her, and is up for hours, unable to calm down, turning on every light. We find her sitting at her little table, wrapping a stick she picked up from the park with masking tape. Speaking in a high voice, as if she is sleepwalking. I strip her, dress her in shorts and a tank, give her water and animal crackers. Her father sleeps on the floor of her room. I bring the baby into bed. But then I am unable to get back to sleep. And the next day, and all those days, amid Zoom classes and student conferences, I sleepwalk through the day. Almost broken with no sleep, my friend texts me that January. Her husband has stayed inside the bedroom for two weeks as she has taken care of the child, who has not been sleeping. None of our children are sleeping. I wonder if they can sense our unease.

Often, during a day that seems to resemble night, while nursing the baby, I find myself staring at the stuffed snowy owl that my aunt sent us when the baby was born. My aunt, the medievalist, wrote me at the time that the owl was a nod to the symbol of Athena, the warrior goddess, because the baby's name means "wise warrior" in Old English (actually, sort of, she wrote, it's more in Old High German and the Scandinavian languages, as I suspect you already knew, which of course I didn't, although I appreciated the care of the gesture). The owl stares out at me from the bookcase in the front room near the block area, which used to hold my books and now holds their toys. Looking at it now, I remember that the image of an owl also portends death, like a memento mori. I want to put it away in a drawer or a basket so I don't have to look at it. Sometimes with the despair, lately, I can't even breathe. I feel the weight of it on me at night. How extremely isolated and boxed in I begin to feel, at this point in that winter. After Joseph Cornell's brother and mother had died, and he was in his house alone, sometimes he would fold the front half of his body in a heated oven, just to feel warmth. I think of Cornell in his nocturnal isolation, like his owls. But surrounded by his forest materials, assembling his boxes in his cellar, in his nestingness, there was a "warm and redolent atmosphere."

The snow, even when it keeps us inside, is still beautiful. My daughter putting on a snowsuit and chasing outside after its disappearance. Sometimes I sleep in, then stumble out to a village. The train tracks in the middle of the room; the translucent rainbow tiles, like stained glass, are helicopter pads. I am making a city, she says. In a letter from 1963, Cornell wrote: "Despite deluge of . . . never-ending crises I cannot refrain from attempting communicating to you the great joys that unfold in our little quarter-acre." This was two years before his brother died, and one year later his mother would follow, and then he was alone in that house, in his grief. I think of the flashes of joy, in all of the various constellations of a rich life of the interior, despite crises, both spectacular and ordinary, despite the solitude of this grief.

The snow is so beautiful. I watch it from the window. It falls so fast. The baby is asleep on me. Her body is changing. The circle of fat at her wrist is disappearing. Soon she will be toddling after her sister, building cities. What light, I wonder, will they remember from this time? What light will I?

THE HALL OF OCEAN LIFE

The Vortex

The following fall, during the short November holiday, my older daughter turns five. Her father is sick—he's never sick—a fever, cough, nausea. He shuts himself in the bedroom to nap, shuffling out to pee, to eat a banana or a few bites of toast, to make himself tea. We keep taking at-home tests, for him, for the kindergartener, so that she can return to school. Money is tight this time of year, but I buy three boxes at Duane Reade. So far negative. Last week I was the one sick, or at least run-down, itchy ghost maps of shingles around my left torso, a side effect, I suspect, of the booster. I guzzled coffee to stay focused during incessant Zooms, eyes blurry from the glare of the gleaming cube. While I try to work, the children play with a plastic medical kit, their dolls in makeshift hospital beds. I find one on a radiator later that day, warm to the touch. The baby wanders around giving shots. Next week her sister will finally get the vaccine. Her sister, who yells out to her—Nurse, nurse, come here! We need to x-ray—as she places two cork yoga blocks on top of a doll, making an electric zizzing sound: Clear! Her baby sister toddles over and stands watch. They don't realize that I'm now taking a video of them from the couch. When they do, they climb on top of me, grabbing the phone.

I keep taking these videos of my children, out of a desire to remember their kinetic movements, their moments of absorption in play. The baby is teething, her last sets of little fangs protruding, the canines top and bottom, red-faced, drooling, though still in fairly good spirits. At night I drag the crib out to the living room so her father can sweatily occupy the bed alone. She's up every two hours. Like a dummy I give her my breast each time, even though it hurts—her latch slipping out, my nipple a red angry point—because I know it offers her relief. As I'm now responsible for feeding the children, I carve up halves of an overly ripe avocado, shake out broken crackers, spoonfuls of yogurt with fruit, the last slices of the forty-dollar pumpkin pie I bought, trying to have something of a Thanksgiving. The suckers from a leftover party bag. Anything in the cabinet the kid can reach. When have I last left the house? Or bathed? When have the days felt a certain division from night?

I occasionally send friends videos and photographs of my children, just to have something to communicate. Impossible to show the pace of these days. The labor of caretaking while working multiple jobs. How any sickness slows. The girls' strep last month, then the older one's serum sickness from the antibiotics. Feels like it was already a year ago. The vortex, my friend Bhanu calls it. Have been in the vortex, we write to each other, when there's been an absence. The photographs don't really tell anything—they are just flashes of light.

Calendar

For her birthday, I promise my daughter I will take her to the natural history museum to see the dinosaurs. Although it's difficult lately to orient ourselves in time, we remember that it's been almost a year since she's seen them, since we visited with her friend for his birthday, two weeks after hers. I remember her mask with the dinosaur print getting wet in the freezing rain. I remember the baby asleep on me, pressing against each other through damp wool. I remember the two children holding hands pointing at the fossils in the display cases, pointing up at the massive dinosaur bones of the T. rex, then at one point running around and around, around and around, so fast they were a blur, stripping themselves of their parkas, scarves, mittens. Afterward the children climbed a tree in Central Park, a new terrain for them after meeting so often in Prospect Park. They clutch the toy dinosaurs bought for them at the emptied-out gift shop, their snow boots swinging above us. Strange to think that was all one year ago. Now her little sister is clutching last year's dinosaur, staggering around and roaring, which we laugh at, a relief.

Last year, at the gift shop, they were giving away a brand-new dinosaur calendar, a replacement for the one already hanging in our kitchen, now nearing its final month. When the cashier handed it to my daughter, who of course wanted to keep it, I thought of a similar dinosaur calendar, one used by David Wojnarowicz in 1989 as he was living with AIDS, the illness to which he had lost his mentor and former lover Peter Hujar two years earlier. I have been thinking about this calendar since encountering it in person in his archives the winter that I was pregnant, right before the pandemic. I had first seen this calendar years ago in an exhibit curated by Julie Ault, and now look at it again online—the calendar open to June, crowded with reminders of his friends (their birthdays, their art shows, sometimes just their names), written in his tender all-capped scrawl in thin black marker, orange pencil, and black and red pen, animated with his arrows and underlining: errands, an ACT UP action at City Hall, plans for a trip or trips, movies to see, a note to watch an interview with Jean Genet filmed right before his death being shown at 10 p.m. on channel 13, and, of course, doctor's appointments.

I found the calendar, then as now, deeply moving: the traces of the artist's hand, the ephemera of his embodied life, all of the mostly indecipherable notations of days that proceed even amid crisis. How plainly it charts the transience of life and marks the cruelty of its brevity during a plague—even more resonant now, with so many lives lost, so many grieving the absences of intimacies that once proceeded in all their smallness and dailiness. Now, years into another pandemic, when thinking of these twin dinosaur calendars, I experience a sensation of time collapsing— a familiar feeling now, as months begin to layer on top of each other, the pace of these days impossible to communicate, the labor of caretaking for two small children while working multiple jobs. In the 1989 calendar, June is illustrated with images of the prehistoric apex ocean predators known as water beast lizards, fierce fanged creatures with long necks undulating out of the blue water. A flash from last winter: the long gentle neck of my daughter's apatosaurus peeking over the rim of the bathtub. I kept wanting to photograph it but never managed to do so.

At the gift shop this year, as additional birthday presents, my daughter carefully selects a quartz crystal and a dinosaur flashlight that comes with a set of miniature ring slides that can be used to project illustrations of dinosaurs, or photographs of their bones, onto her bedroom ceiling. She often carries the flashlight when we walk the dog in the early evening, once I've finished teaching for the day. I have often wondered about children's fascination with dinosaurs, whether they are aware of the melancholy of their extinction. Scrolling through the digitized archive of Wojnarowicz's work available online, I saw the same fascination in his collections: all the toy dinosaurs and reptilian figures he kept as talismans from an otherwise unhappy childhood. I have begun to understand that his affinity for these extinct creatures was part of his attention to the small and the cosmic, that this historical awareness and planetary despair exists alongside his mourning and caretaking of loved ones and his reckoning with his own diagnosis.

Last year, jittery in an enclosed public space, I fed my daughter on a bench downstairs, in the light near the staff entrance, while museum workers kept approaching and pointing me to a nursing room, which I kept declining. This year, in a darkened auditorium at the museum, I breastfeed our new baby while half watching a video of mass extinctions, listening to the strangely soothing narration of its timeline.

We keep the free dinosaur calendar, cut it up to make collages, always in search of a craft project. That winter we return to the old pattern of staying mostly indoors, mindful of the threat of a new variant, a rhythm of heightened vigilance and isolation to which we've grown accustomed.

Birthday

We're now entering yet another pandemic winter. Already an almost nothingness of snow flurries that quickly dissipate. I look up and again the trees are almost bare. Leaves occasionally float down outside the window. On walks, they crunch beneath our feet. That sweet-turning-sour smell of rotting leaves, their dulling palette.

The day before my daughter's birthday is also the anniversary of Peter Hujar's death, an event that will catalyze, for Wojnarowicz, an intense period of thinking and artmaking, a time of elegiac contemplation also rooted in a sustained attention to the natural world. I keep thinking about a moment documented in his diary, when he moves into Hujar's loft after his death, the space where he had helped care for him, and realizes it's winter only after he discovers that brown leaves have been filling the bathtub, falling through an open window. That is how grief works—slow and then fast. That is how time seems to work now. Yet the seasons still cycle through, insistently.

That same week is also my mother's birthday. Almost twenty years have passed since her death, since I sat by her side, holding her hand. Hujar and my mother were almost the same age when they died, one of AIDS, the other of cancer, each after a short and devastating illness. I wonder if I'm drawn to both Wojnarowicz and Hujar in part because they remind me of my mother, born at a certain time, their childhoods of a mysterious and mythical privation between small-town or rural New Jersey and New York City, dead tragically at what should have been the middle of their lives. I don't know why it is causing me so much pain this year. Still, after two decades. When I tell her I have been weeping all day, my sister sends me long-stemmed yellow roses, my mother's favorite. The flowers look absurd, funereal, in the chaos of the room where we do all of our living. Still, I know it's the gesture. I tell my daughter they are for her, for her birthday, but to celebrate her grandmother as well. In his journal, Wojnarowicz bemoaned the arrival of so many flowers after the funeral. His friend surprised him by insisting on Catholic rites, and he writes of desiring another language and experience outside of these received spoken forms, a spirituality that actually confronts death, "the whole mystery of it the fears and joys of it." I realize that I keep returning to this artist, and the way he documented mourning as a form of witness, because there is much to grieve now, so many dead without ceremony, and often no space or rituals in which to do so.

The Uses of Sorrow

In the January before the shutdown, feeling unbearably nauseous early in my still-secret second pregnancy, I took the Q train to Union Square and walked to the Fales Library at NYU, to sit in the reading room and contemplate Wojnarowicz's notebook and to try to find the fragments of his unfinished film. I was preparing to give a talk at Harvard about the forms of grief in his work, which I saw as ecological—that is, concerning both the individual and the collective, the human and the nonhuman. In his notebook, in an intensely beautiful passage that he will lift almost entirely for the title essay in his memoir *Close to the Knives*, he writes of the hospital beds where he has sat, waiting for his friends to die, and the rituals he feels compelled to perform at the death of the man he calls "my brother, my father, my emotional link to the world"—slowly panning across his body with his Super 8 film camera, capturing him in a series of still photographs. I finally find the transferred footage on a DVD entitled "Mexico, etc. Peter etc." The sharper features of Hujar's postmortem face and his slender, elegant hand, like something out of an El Greco crucifixion, taking me back to the hands I have held on hospital beds as those I have loved have taken their last breaths. In the intimacy of the deathbed images, Wojnarowicz is channeling Hujar's portraits. Now processing his own vast archive of negatives in his mentor's darkroom, Wojnarowicz begins to conjure his alchemy of tone and shadow.

At Fales, I order up Wojnarowicz's personal copy of *Portraits in Life and Death*, the only photography book Hujar published in his lifetime, with its introduction by his friend Susan Sontag, written from a hospital bed after her surgery for recently diagnosed breast cancer. In this book Hujar presents the photographs he took in the 1960s of the skeletal remains in the Sicilian catacombs, juxtaposing them with portraits of his friends, such as John Waters and Sontag, posed lying down, both a contemplative pose and a rehearsal of their own mortality. Witnessing Hujar's death, and choosing to record both this and his mourning, was a catalyst for the younger artist, while revealing a heightened awareness that he too was going to die, although he would have years instead of months. It also evinced his desire to document a mystical experience, an homage to his friend that would give him back the grace and dignity that the hysterical fear of contagion and homophobia had denied him in his final months. How do we go on living and making art, in the face of so much death?

I think of the poem by Mary Oliver, "The Uses of Sorrow":

> Someone I loved once gave me
> A box full of darkness
>
> It took me years to understand
> that this, too, was a gift.

In his elegies to his chosen family, as well as the creatures and landscapes Wojnarowicz encounters—in these paragraphs and photographs—we are given boxes of darkness as well as light.

The Bardo

In his journal, Wojnarowicz writes of his wish to make a film of "the process of grief," something associative and intuitive, a desire to record impressions, especially outside in nature, trying to see the world through his camera as his friend did. At the end of the third day after Hujar's death, likely after consulting Hujar's copy of The Tibetan Book of the Dead, he notes that it was time for the spirit to leave the body, in the porous in-between of the bardo. Earlier that day, or perhaps the day before—time blurs in the grief journal—he travels to Hujar's grave at Gate of Heaven in Westchester County. During that drive, on a gray rainy day through a dirty windshield, he takes on his mentor's gaze, his play with and use of darkness in his photographs, seeing in the bird nests high in the trees "everything rich and black and brown the serious rich black of his photographs almost wet looking." He walks around the cemetery trying to find Hujar's floating soul, which he imagines as a powerful white light. He drives on the turnpike to the Great Swamp in New Jersey, bringing with him his loaded Super 8 camera to shoot on impulse. As a child, the ponds and streams and woods of New Jersey had been a sanctuary for Wojnarowicz, a refuge from a brutal home life. Now, in his grief and a desire to transcend his present moment, he immerses himself in the natural world. He senses his friend everywhere, dissipated through the atmosphere. In his ecstatic descriptions of walking around one of the only virgin forests left in the state, he sees a "primordial place where dinosaurs once slept." He turns on the camera and starts running, shooting bursts of film, jumping over fallen branches. He sees a stream and, setting up the camera, strips off his clothes and begins splashing himself with water. Once he gets dressed, he takes the camera and starts spinning under the canopy of trees, and the heavy gray storm clouds, recalling, when writing about the experience later, dancing around and around with a friend, the artist Kiki Smith, in front of open windows during a rainstorm at the loft, in an ecstatic expression of grief—how the curtains twisted like veils, he remembers, a liturgical image. The writing is filled with his characteristic propulsion, like the whirling around he is describing:

> whirling beneath the trees the light and grey-filled sky the clouds becoming patchy and animal—trained the lens on fragments of water surface containing sky and trees and broke the surface with pale hands rubbing sediments broken dark leaves cold clean water over my hands. Whirled again; chased mammal height the surface of the forest floor spinning around trees and rolled over and over among them.

For a while, I found it devastating that this film was unfinished. Over time, however, I've realized that for Wojnarowicz these fragments were less about a finished work and more about the private ritual, a longing to contemplate beauty and joy amid individual and collective crisis, including the loss felt by ecological spoilage and changes in the landscape. The philosopher Glenn Albrecht used the term "solastalgia" to refer to the distress caused by environmental change, a sense of a home to which one can never completely return. In this film, and in his notebooks circling around both personal and ecological grief, Wojnarowicz is paying tribute to his friend, to Hujar's journeys to see beauty in the tarnished or unlovely, frequently returning to their native New Jersey or traveling to upstate New York to take photographs of abandoned buildings and trashed interiors—what Hujar called ruins— and also sensitive portraits of watchful farm animals in fields, like his series of cows staring contemplatively at the camera, a sight he would have been deeply familiar with from growing up on his grandparents' farm. In his film, Wojnarowicz includes footage he took before Hujar's death, tenderly shadowing the photographer, who is seen camera in hand, wearing a puffer vest; we never see the older man's face, only the bald spot visible on the back of his head, as he walks searchingly beneath a highway overpass.

On days when I can escape outside, after uninterrupted hours spent staring at a screen, to go with John and the baby to take the train to pick up our daughter from school, I spend time looking at the becoming-winter sky. The filtered light of cold days, the sky like a milky fluid. The description of clouds in the artist's grief journal are almost pastoral, at the edge of elegy: "patchy and animal," or elsewhere "like gauze like grey overlapping in fog," or "postcard clouds with fire rays of light colliding against the firm shark grey of the horizon." When his fellow artist and activist Zoe Leonard worried whether she should be making more explicitly political work, as opposed to her photographic studies of clouds, taken from airplanes, Wojnarowicz told her not to give up on beauty. This is what they were fighting for, he told her. So that we—as artists, as people, as those struggling for survival—can have beauty again.

I think I look to Wojnarowicz and this elegiac period of his, this time he spent thinking and artmaking, because I am trying to figure out, still, for myself, what beauty can come out of mourning, whether the mourning of others can exist alongside the mourning of a dying planet, and whether it is permissible for this mourning to exist alongside an ecstatic contemplation of the natural world.

Layers of the Ocean

At the museum this year, my daughter stops to consider the exhibits more attentively, asks us to read to her from the placards. Still, like before, she tires out after an hour and wants to go home and eat birthday cake. Like last year, we have saved the Hall of Ocean Life for last. To enter the cavernous structure feels like descending into the ocean, darkness backlit by lights and the glow of the deep-ocean dioramas. I remember, from last time, the din, the sounds of the ocean from the shark video being shown below, the massive central screen its own luminescence.

The drooping manatee floating in its exhibit, as if cognizant of its own current doomed state—unable to find a food supply, as I have just read. We linger in front of the cobalt-blue-hued case, the blurry outline of neon creatures: "In order to survive in this sunless world, 90 percent of all deep-sea animals living below 700 meters have the ability to generate their own light."

Last winter, when we were shut inside, I began to attempt to teach my daughter about the natural world. I thought, if I can teach her about life in the ocean, about the variety of ecosystems, then she will care later on when she learns how greatly it is threatened because of human action. It was a way for me to cope with an ecological sorrow that was beginning to overwhelm me. From a book on oceans, with meditative illustrations of sea creatures, we learned that the ocean is divided into five parts: The Sunlight Zone. The Twilight Zone. The Midnight Zone. The Abyss Zone. The Trench Zone, at the ocean's deepest floor, where light can no longer cut through. While we read, she clutches her blue whale figurine, which glides elegantly under the surface of her bath whenever she drops it in the water.

At the museum I stare at the cloudy blue glass filtering light through the ceiling, and at the suspended massive fiberglass model of the female blue whale, now with a bandage affixed to its side, as the upstairs gallery is being used as a vaccination site. I wonder whether David Wojnarowicz stood beneath this same whale, installed in 1969 when he was fifteen, and feel certain that he would have—that premonitory sense of layered time that I've come to think of as a history feeling, which also permeates so much of his work. In his essay on his friend, the artist begins juxtaposing scenes of Hujar's illness, the inhumanity of his treatment, with a pair of atomistic facts about whales (blue whales, although he doesn't name them). One, that whales can descend to a depth of five thousand feet, where they must sustain a pressure of one hundred and forty tons on their body. The other, that a female blue whale produces more than two hundred liters of milk daily after giving birth. I'm not sure why he chooses to begin his elegy in this way, paralleling these two endangered bodies—perhaps to point to acts of survival and care in the natural world that transcend the human.

In his grief, Wojnarowicz also felt an obsessive drive to film the beluga whales at the Coney Island aquarium, footage that he juxtaposed with his film of his friend's recently deceased body, a mythical sequence for me that I had read about in Cynthia Carr's biography of Wojnarowicz, which led me almost two years ago to his archives at Fales in an attempt to find it. I watched the whales swim around and around in their enclosure, barely turning, resembling the strange fetal shape I had just seen on the monitor of the ultrasound the week before. I felt the vibrations of their bodies. In his journal Wojnarowicz writes about driving on the West Side Highway and through the tunnel into Brooklyn and out to Coney Island, going with Hujar to see the whales on one of their trips to various quack doctors and con men who were promising a cure, and how in their exhaustion they watched them for some time, finding something celestial in their orb-like white shapes, the sun streaming in through the waters. Yet on the first trip to film them, the glass case was emptied of water.

There were just four whales swimming in a shallow pool. Still, in their graceful form and imagined intellect, he writes, all the mysteries of the world were somehow answered.

The Abyss

Through much of last February, snowed in with my daughters, I thought about the beluga whales, about their abbreviated lives in captivity, where so few of their calves survive, and in the wild, the destruction of their coastal habitats, as well as the change to their migration patterns caused by melting sea ice. "I think of Peter I think of those whales I think of sad innocence in the face of death and the turning of this planet," Wojnarowicz wrote. I feel certain that he was contemplating the lives of the whales as well, not just as metaphor or symbol, connecting the grief and vulnerability of humans alongside the nonhuman, their caretaking as paralleling his own.

On YouTube I watch videos of beluga whales nursing, which they can do for up to three years, every half hour. The nipple pops out through a slit, and the calves curl their tongue like a straw, forming a seal, similar to human infants. My little human nurses, rapturously sucking on my nipple, rhythmically dream-feeding—I have to stick my finger in her mouth to detach her, switch her, as I work on my laptop over her. I think of Hujar's series of photographs of the baby John McClellan with his mother, Dina, the close-up of the baby breastfeeding; the mother becomes a landscape, the shadows cast across her breasts, the planetary ink abyss of her lap. The baby's eyes are closed, totally focused and interior, as I gaze down at her head. The rhythm of her sucking, the little sighs, the radiator heat, the humidifier. Time stretches out. Almost a full year later, I am still working with my daughter on me, still in that interior space, but her body stretches across my lap, her knees curling underneath my arm, her legs extended beyond.

That February, the month I have been thinking of as the abyss, I began researching epimeletic behavior—specifically, the mourning of animals, such as beluga whales and other species of cetaceans, who often keep the bodies of their dead calves next to them. Sometimes they use a carcass of another species, or another object, for their mourning rituals; one captive female beluga was observed to focus on a buoy, as a grief object, for several months. They can also mourn collectively, like the members of one pod of endangered killer whales who took turns floating the body of a newborn calf. In 2018, an orca living off the coast of Puget Sound swam for seventeen days and a thousand miles, pushing the dead body of her calf in the water, then diving down to retrieve it. During this time, Bhanu sends me an image of a drawing she made in her notebook of an orca mother and baby, though she knows nothing of my ongoing interest in whale behavior. I was writing you a letter in my head, I wrote to her. Just send it telepathically! she wrote back.

This year, the students in my class on ecological writing partici-
pate from home, many from their childhood rooms. I am teaching
with a new baby, without any maternity leave. I tell them to keep
notebooks, to pay attention to their landscape, the weather, the
creatures they encounter during their neighborhood walks. That
February, many of them write through their grief about the deep
freeze and massive power outage in Texas, how it exposed those
most vulnerable, the parents who struggled to keep their children safe, the eleven-year-old who froze to death in a mobile
home. And also the animals: All the primates who died in the
sanctuary. The thousands of stunned turtles who had to be res-
cued. I was reminded of a moment in Cynthia Carr's biography,
a Christmas when Wojnarowicz and his two siblings were driven
by their father to a five-and-dime shopping center. The children
were given five dollars, which David used to purchase turtles
that he carried home in a take-out container. When their father
forgot to pick them up, they had to walk home on a highway,
through a blizzard, and the young David kept crying, insisting
that they stop in a diner, worried that the turtles had frozen to
death. Even when he got older, he would steal lizards and turtles
from pet shops and let them free in Central Park. I think of Hujar's photograph of a shirtless David holding a garter snake while
sitting against a tree, grinning and relaxed, like a kid in the outdoors. In Wojnarowicz's own photographs, always an attention
to the small and unloved of the animal world, insects and reptiles.
There is a famous photograph of his hand holding the tiniest of
frogs, the overlaid text wondering, in his intense philosophical
way, what this small creature's role is in the world. "If this little
guy dies does the world know? Does the world feel this?" As

with the whales, in his empathy he is thinking through suffering and mortality and caring for even the most miniature of beings, what the philosopher Donna Haraway calls "making kin." In a passage in Wojnarowicz's grief journal, he describes driving on the highway to the Great Swamp, and suddenly seeing a pack of stray dogs standing around the body of another dog recently struck by a car, the scene lit by the red taillights: "In the driving snow they sniffed at his form unwilling to leave it behind." I think about mourning as witness, the care work, that animals can also perform for each other.

The Thing Illuminated

At the Hall of Ocean Life, walking around with the kids, I use my phone to photograph details of the sky and horizon in the backpainting of the dioramas, each set in a specific place and during a particular time of day. The dawn-like golden light of the sun, the bursts of pink and purple clouds like cotton candy at sunset. The skies set off from the quality of light underneath the aqua water. John takes a video for me, panning across the tuna fish and dolphins under the water, and the flying fish stilled in flight above the warped layer of translucent plastic marking the water's surface. The diorama is all stillness, but the movement of the camera creates a quality of activity—teeming schools of fish, flocks of birds in the morning air. The heavy backdrop of clouds layered with choppy gray above a herd of walruses. I stop in front of the diorama showing the aftermath of a polar bear stalking a ribbon seal, focusing on the striated sunset light filtering through layered dense clouds, grayer than the blue-tinged icy landscape. Since the 1960s, I read online, the polar bear's head has been turned toward the viewer, as if to try to meet our gaze. As I try to stare back at the polar bear, I think of the encounter in W. G. Sebald's *The Rings of Saturn* between the narrator and the stuffed polar bear at the entrance hall of the ruined Somerleyton Hall: "With its yellowish and moth-eaten fur, it resembles a ghost bowed by sorrows." This solitary creature that traveled miles every day of its life, mapping out its own internal cartography, is now cramped forever inside this box. Because of the melting of ice in the sea, its descendants must travel even farther to hunt.

Earlier this month, in the weekly lecture I'm teaching this year in a literature class on "The Animal," we watch a video of a polar bear emerging from the hibernation of her maternity den with her cubs, then rolling down a snowy hill with them, as if sledding. We watch the clip over and over, a moment of joy and ease in a Zoom where so often I teach to squares of darkness. This year the undergraduates are shut up in their dorm rooms, alienated after two years of isolation, and often I don't know how to reach them. Polar bears spend the most time together in the wild during the three years the mother nurses her cub. I wonder what my fascination is with these solitary immense creatures, who nurse their young for so long. I think of last February, when we were snowed in for weeks, not able to shovel ourselves out so that we could go sledding in the park or even take a walk. I didn't leave the house for days. I remember the blinding light of the blizzard. In my ecological writing class that February we read Annie Dillard meditating on the light of a snowfall in *Pilgrim at Tinker Creek*:

> It snowed. It snowed all yesterday and never emptied the sky, although the clouds looked so low and heavy they might drop all at once with a thud. The light is diffuse and hueless, like the light on paper inside a pewter bowl. The snow looks light and the sky dark, but in fact the sky is lighter than the snow. Obviously the thing illuminated cannot be lighter than its illuminator.

While we are snowed in, I watch my daughter build a winter scene above the cool glow of her lightbox: a small red panda, tiny plastic penguins, her bath-toy polar bear, translucent tiles for icicles. Later that month I am finally able to score a polar bear figurine I've been trying to find, from the German toy company Schleich, an item that was sold out for some time. The top review of the polar bear is from someone who has placed it on her mother's grave as seen in an accompanying photograph. It was her mother's favorite animal, she writes, as it was her high school mascot.

Sea and Fog

In 1976, two years after he arrived in New York City, Hiroshi Sugimoto came to the American Museum of Natural History to photograph the polar bear diorama. The film he used was black-and-white, removing the exhibit's unnatural coloration, transforming the fake painted backdrop and the red-painted blood splattered across the snow. When looking at dioramas, the photographer has said, he made a discovery: the taxidermied animals and painted backdrops looked fake, but when he looked at them while closing one eye, all perspective vanished and they looked real, like looking at the world through a camera. My mind travels to Wojnarowicz's photograph of bison falling off a cliff, taken a decade after Sugimoto's—a photo of a diorama at the natural history museum in Washington, D.C., the animals transformed into almost abstract, biomorphic black forms. The photograph is often read as a response to the senseless speed at which lives were lost during the AIDS crisis, but in this image I believe he is also linking the time he is living and dying in to the devastation of the past, not only the extinction of the buffalo by white hunters but also the elimination of a way of life for the Plains Indians, who regarded the buffalo, and their hunting, as sacred. Wojnarowicz's gaze, his planetary despair, lingers there, suspended, a historical weight.

The fog-like backdrop of Sugimoto's photograph of the polar bear diorama, blurring where the snow meets the sky, reminds me of his seascapes, which become studies in atmosphere and time. Sometimes the horizon is just a line, at other times it disappears—the horizon suggestive, as the artist has said, of the ocean's deep time, this vision remaining across billions of years, despite how humans have otherwise altered the landscape. Sometimes, in viewing one of Sugimoto's seascapes, one stares at the blur into darkness, like an abyss.

Because the poet and painter Etel Adnan has just died, I also think, while staring at the backdrops of the dioramas, of her love of the horizon, its perfect line where it meets the sea or as it is disrupted by mountains, a repeated subject of her paintings. From one of her poems:

> *Humanity is an ocean, each person a bubble, appearing, disappearing, and reappearing on its turn.*

And for us now, at this moment of history, what is beyond the horizon?

At the Hall of Ocean Life, we sit down on the floor to watch a video. Amid a crowd, staring at the screen or at the cloudy blue glass overhead, I nurse the baby in the carrier while my now five-year-old leans against me, taking a quick break from her mask for one long inhale. For that brief period, we are piled comfortably on top of one another, watching the movements of the deep. There is this feeling of being underwater, yet with wriggling children in place of schools of fish. All at once, I feel an overwhelming sensation of life's fragility and eternity. We are alive, I think, for just a moment of all of this.

TIME DUST—BLACK HOLE

a meditation on grayness

On a Saturday afternoon in March, the day before the first day of spring, we decided to get in the car and travel from Brooklyn to the lower part of Manhattan. Traveling together was still a necessity at this point—we hadn't figured out how to separate, so we went together everywhere, as a pack. I was trying to locate the area called Coenties Slip, where in the middle of the last century a loose community of painters lived in illegal warehouse lofts, among them Ellsworth Kelly, Robert Indiana, and Agnes Martin. When Martin moved out of the third floor of 3-5 Coenties Slip to a studio nearby, the young painter James Rosenquist moved in, and while living there he began his first series of paintings inspired by the atmosphere and conversations about abstraction. I had been commissioned to write about a thirty-five-foot painting in grayscale, or grisaille, by Rosenquist entitled *Time Dust–Black Hole*. The painting was to be exhibited at the end of April, but I was invited to view it earlier in the month at an art storage facility in Newark, which necessitated another family trip. Feeling anxious about the commission, and in general burned out from overwork, I wanted to walk around Coenties Slip, to think about grayness and collage, and how this all has to do with the city—with something like an elegiac gaze, as this was a sensibility I was told I shared with the artist. John was always ready to go somewhere and think about painting and, as usual when seeing art these days, we promised the girls a playground and ice cream. I wanted to be walking around the city, something I hadn't been able to do in the past two years, perhaps even since I'd had my children; to think about space, how a painting can take up space, but also how my own writing occurs within space and time, in deep space, in deep time. In the grimness of that March, I was also attempting to search for what could make me, in this current state of numbness and emptiness, feel alive.

I had become interested in the eerie incongruities of this part of the city, its layered history that is discordant with the rest of the tight grid, like a fragment in a collage. I imagined initially while doing my research that I would be walking around in solitude. I would circumambulate the city on a dreamy Sabbath afternoon, walking its edge like the wanderlustful sailor Ishmael at the beginning of Melville's *Moby-Dick*, who walks past points of commerce on the shoreline, past docked ships and thousands of sailors, from the shipbuilding center of production at Corlears Hook, where women serviced the sailors—the apparent origin of the term "hooker"—to Coenties Slip, once a boisterous waterfront along the East River. (The term "slip" refers to a manmade berth for a boat, the triangular shape of Coenties determined by the shoreline's curve.) From there to Pearl Street, so named by the Dutch for the shells and pearls discarded on the riverbank by the Lenape, piled several feet high, as the New

York harbor then was once home to half the world's oysters. The day before, I'd read all I could about the development of the harbor, how the city has been building out into the water since the Dutch colonial days in the 1600s, creating new land by sticking wooden frames in the river muck and then filling the interior with junk rock and garbage, the buildings standing on landfill, the city created into the water. Coenties Slip, along Pearl Street, made up parts of what we know today as Water, Front, and South streets, all consecutively filled in over the centuries. During the late nineteenth century, the warehouses here supplied the nautical industries; the streets were lined with gasworks and supply shops, stores for tackle and netting, ropes and sailcloth and other bricolage that could still be found in the artists' lofts more than half a century later, and that sometimes appeared in their paintings. There was, as Nancy Princenthal writes in her biography of Agnes Martin, a profound sense of uncanniness to the riverfront enclave, totally isolated from the city, a strange disjunction between the towers of the nearby financial district and the ramshackle buildings of the old waterfront, the strong smell of salt water, the drunken sailors at night, the bustle of the wholesale fish market that arrived by midcentury. The spacious lofts with high ceilings facing the river had splintered floors and lacked not only kitchens but also hot water and heat; the artists had to hide their beds because of the constant threat of visits from housing authorities. The artists, some of whom became renowned, later spoke of the romantic sense of being out of time in that setting, a sense of community but also privacy, being left alone—both in terms of, for many of them, their queerness, and also in that such surroundings allowed them to live simply as artists, without having to produce paintings consistently, or at least having to make much money at it. James Rosenquist, who arrived at Coenties Slip in 1960, remembered collecting copies of *Life* magazine in his loft, writing ideas on the wall in pencil, engaging more in thinking about painting than in painting, trying to imagine an abstraction that might come from painting objects in various scales, as he had learned to do from his union job painting billboards. He was interested in the juxtaposition of disparate images, chosen for form and color rather than content, such as the bundles of pencils that reappear in his work (as in the painting I have been asked to think through) like memories floating in from childhood, pencils that seem weaponized, transformed into aircraft, while also existing in their original wood-and-graphite form. In this later painting, *Time Dust–Black Hole*, the artist is reviving the gray palette he used during this early period—his interest in grayscale shared by fellow artists there, such as Jasper Johns, who lived nearby on Pearl Street, investigating the materiality of gray, or Agnes Martin, discovering the fragile and subtle graphite line of the pencil in the grid paintings she began making at Coenties Slip. Thinking of this, I wonder yet again if the painting I was asked to meditate upon was in part a thesis on abstraction, a painting that was an essay on painting.

In the viewing room I was led to at the storage facility in Newark, I was able to observe up close the various textures of the massive painting, made up of seven panels, drips approximating galaxy dust that seemed impishly Pollockian, a black hole at the center panel that might reference Ad Reinhardt. For Rosenquist, grisaille becomes a void, the void of color allowing the objects depicted to become mere forms, to develop space. The grayscale objects in the painting—a can, a penny, a French horn, the small sailboat at the edge perhaps like the aluminum speedboat he built from plans in *Popular Mechanics*, which looked to the child growing up in northern Minnesota like a rocket ship—appear reflective, metallic, like the flicker of chrome, even more so in the cold atmosphere of the art storage facility, sterile and hermetically sealed, me alone in the room with just the painting, lying down on the gray concrete floor, as if I were in outer space, yet still in a facility that stored art as frozen capital, waiting for value to accrue through museum retrospectives, gallery shows, or critical examination, such as I am embarking upon here. While writing this, I think of the artist discussing how his paintings were often commissioned for corporate environments, and the ambivalence these commissions inspired, the sense that he was supposed to give them something and he was unsure of what—a kinship I feel walking around thinking of this painting, that perhaps the artist himself would be okay with the various digressions this writing commission has inspired, that perhaps these digressions could even be understood as a way to create in writing something like the effects of collage—a "hallucinatory realism," as he writes of his work, disrupting the pictorial plane.

It is on a gray day that I make it to Coenties Slip, family in tow, with the intention of walking around the area, the clouds still shot through with light, a grayness that the painter Jack Youngerman, who lived in the lofts, referred to as "pigeon gray," as where the gray of sky and buildings meets the darker gray of the river. I think of the iconic black-and-white 1958 photograph by

Hans Namuth of a group of these artists on the roof of 3-5 Coenties Slip, "the gray masonry of old office towers," Princenthal notes, "massed behind them," three of the male painters—Robert Indiana, Ellsworth Kelly, and Jack Youngerman—standing around the young cherubic son Youngerman shared with the actress Delphine Seyrig, who is sitting on a broken Adirondack chair, watching her toddler attentively, as Agnes Martin, hands in the pockets of her white coat, watches from the other side. Looking at this photograph now, I think of what it must have been like to raise a small child in an artist's loft, perhaps without hot water, and of how Seyrig must have bathed her child, as I have just done, on a gray Sunday in early April, washing her hair weekly, the bathtub water leaving a gray ring of dirt that then must be scrubbed out, the fulfillment of this ritual somehow satisfying yet also monotonous—all of which reminds me in turn of Seyrig's role as the Belgian widowed housewife in Chantal Akerman's film *Jeanne Dielman, 23 quai du Commerce, 1080 Bruxelles*. Many of the artists who lived here showered nearby at the Seamen's Church Institute's old location on South Street, although Agnes Martin had a clawfoot bathtub in her bedroom. The eldest of the group (she was forty-five at the time of that 1958 photo), besides her close friend and probable lover the weaver Lenore Tawney, from Lorain, Ohio, Martin would bake muffins in a cast-iron kitchen stove and host Ellsworth Kelly for breakfast every morning.

We find parking near a small park with a sign that says ODD SLIP, and since the baby is asleep in the car, I leave her with her father, who is working on a review on his phone. With me comes the five-year-old, who insists on bringing a small notebook and pencil with her, so that she can also take notes, although she has yet to learn how to write, making instead a series of wavy lines with the pencil. I am happy to have her with me, as my walking and thinking companion. It is always easier when we are outside. I follow the map of my research from the day before. We begin walking down one block, past massive bank buildings and corporate towers, including a structure housing JPMorgan Chase, a company whose origins trace back to the Bank of Manhattan, founded at the end of the eighteenth century by Aaron Burr, and which profited off the aftermath of the city poisoning its own water supply. Herman Melville was born at number 6 Pearl Street; a Starbucks now sits across the road. The buildings where the artists lived have been mostly demolished to make way for these high-rise developments, until the landmarked tavern block at Pearl Street, where nineteenth-century brick buildings in the Federal style have been allowed to stand. I think again of "circumambulate," Melville's term, as I walk around and around the block of fairly dilapidated brick and granite warehouses, clutching the hand of my child, who is pleased to be out with me in the world on an adventure, her chin still bandaged from where she split it open the weekend before, prompting a series of visits to urgent cares, pediatric ERs, a pediatric dentist, and a plastic surgeon consult during the week of my spring break. The visit to the dentist produced a strange black-and-white image of adult teeth crowding on top of tiny baby teeth that reminds me perversely of real estate development.

We walk around and around the same deli, pizza place, fish-and-chips shop, a modern-looking but dystopian-seeming bone broth place—everything empty, as it is the weekend, so there are no workers from the financial district getting lunch. Many of the storefronts have been boarded up, as tourists and workers alike have largely been absent now for two years. The streets still smell of stale beer from St. Patrick's Day, and cigarette butts dot the ground. Finally we find a depressing business park with a small sign reading COENTIES SLIP, lined with red metal tables and chairs that no one is occupying, although a man in athletic wear is on his cell phone nearby while picking up after two chihuahuas, and a woman on the bench is arguing with an invisible person over earbuds. We walk around and around, my daughter climbing up on the concrete ledge of what is now the Vietnam Veterans Memorial Plaza; the only color we see in the landscape, besides corporate signage, is the frail pink of new cherry blossom trees. Crossing the street back into Coenties Slip, we are almost hit by a delivery biker speeding to make his quota. After waiting for tacos from a cart inside a coffee shop, no one but us wearing a mask, we try to walk east toward the harbor, near the Staten Island Ferry, but our path is obstructed by a highway. My daughter asks me why I am taking pictures of trash, although the neighborhood is strangely clean, unlike ours in Brooklyn, the trash cans everywhere adorned with the phrase DO YOU DOWNTOWN, not even a question. When we round back into Coenties Slip, the red chairs and tables have been mysteriously taken down. All we can see are expensive-looking people wearing expensive-looking athletic wear and walking small, expensive-looking dogs, most likely financial workers living in one of the high-rises. The only signs of the area's nautical past are planters shaped like boats

outside of S&P Global at 55 Water Street, the old site of the
Whitney Museum of American Art.

We walk back to the car, where I nurse the baby, who is now up
from her nap, sitting happily on her father's lap, and then we
head down as a family to the Battery, where we pay for tickets for
the SeaGlass Carousel, in the site of the old aquarium. Following
a group of older, unmasked women, we all climb into seats shaped
like gigantic, luminescent plastic fish, the baby buckled in with
me, and we proceed to circle around and around. I'm not sure the
baby enjoys the experience, which made even me feel a bit sea-
sick. Later we walk to the water's edge and stare, after Melville,
at the crowds of water gazers, at the blue-green statue that always looks gray in the distance, and at Ellis Island, as a group of
frat boys wonder if it is safe to swim in the East River. I don't
answer them, that no, probably not, though in the past few years
dolphins have been spotted swimming there, as I mention to
John later. By now the grayness has begun to burn off to something approaching noontime sun, as if spring were finally emerging from winter, and it is suddenly so bright and hot that I borrow
my child's too-snug baseball cap to shield myself from sunburn.
I think of the beginning of the audio essay *On Vanishing Land*, a
collaboration between Mark Fisher and Justin Barton I'd listened
to the day before, that documents their walk along the coast of Suffolk, England. Something of a rejoinder to Sebald's treatment of
Suffolk in *The Rings of Saturn*, the essay marks their desire to
meditate on place and the local, past ruins of war and commerce,
attempting to still find natural beauty in the landscape. "This is

April but it feels like summer," the trancelike pilgrimage begins, before moving on to the abstract spaces of sky, sea, and land, the effects of the sea like a liquid wall, a coastal history that also includes fending off incursions. As the collaborators walk to the Felixstowe container port, they observe other buildings of late-stage capitalism, such as a failed luxury hotel since converted into flats. Standing near the river's edge, looking out into the harbor, John and I discuss Agnes Martin saying that you wouldn't think of form when looking at the ocean—her desire for a painting without forms or references. Although Rosenquist's canvases are filled with images, I realize now that his project also deals with nothingness and emptiness, but does so by using images that are drained of associations, he explained, like being drained of color. The images he employs are there simply to develop space, images as pure form.

After the harbor we walk, somewhat dazed, into the growing crowds of tourists and weekend-havers, many seemingly congregating by or emerging from the ferry terminal, until we find ourselves at a playground; John notices it is almost entirely made from stone. I read later that this is marketed as a playground for future children, stormproof, built above sea level, and made mostly of granite. A group of laughing teenagers hurtles down a series of gray slides nearby, including one very high slide; my daughter, with her wounded chin, insists on climbing up and going down the slides, until finally, after the fourth or fifth time, nervous that she might have another accident with such a fresh wound, we tell her to stop. My life lately consists of so many playgrounds with black rubber floors, so many metallic slides, a series of metallic slides in my dreams. In a bid to extract the girls from the playground, I promise them ice cream, and we find ourselves walking, exhausted and overheated, through the deserted byways of Wall Street, as empty on a weekend as when Bartleby lived there, refusing to do any more writing, wanting only to stand and look out the window, with glazed eyes, completely alone in the universe, a bit of a wreck in the mid-Atlantic, as Melville writes. A crowd of younger people, wearing white T-shirts, covered from head to toe in pastel powdered pigment, make their way toward us, and I realize that this is the festival of Holi, their appearance a welcome infusion of color in an otherwise dreary landscape. We carry on to the South Street Seaport—which would feel like a charming-enough mall if not for the hideousness of the chain stores and tourist traps—because we need coffee and also want to visit the new McNally Jackson bookstore, where I hope to find books by Mark Fisher. They have none at that location, however, and I think ruefully of Herman Melville wandering into one of the many antiquarian bookstores that used to be in this area and finding on sale there a copy of Burton's *Anatomy of Melancholy* that had once belonged to his father. Later, as John runs to the car to feed the parking meter, I take the girls to get ice cream, wearing the toddler on me in a carrier, all of us strangely sunburnt, despite the grayness, and find myself delighted by the sight of children with families waiting for ice cream, all covered in blue and pink and yellow, on their cheeks, in their hair. I chat with a mother in line behind me, whose pastel-splattered children in the stroller have, it turns out, the same age gap as mine. As we leave, I take photographs of the splattered pastels on the brick outside, a flash of my daughter's beaten-up metallic pink sneakers making their way into the frame.

While sitting outside the bookstore, I watch a tall ship docked in the harbor—the property, I learn later, of the historical museum next door—and think of the floating sensation of the tiny ship in the painting I am supposed to write about. I wonder if this might be a reference to Joseph Cornell's first collage, a black-and-white image, possibly inspired by Max Ernst, of a clipper ship whose sails give way to a rose containing a spiderweb. As I write this, I think of Sofia's suggestion to me that Sebald's collaged prose is like a Cornell box, both of them steeped in setting, something that suggests a care or attachment to the object. For Cornell, whom the young James Rosenquist would visit in his hermitage in Flushing, Queens, that first collage was autobiographical, gesturing toward his esteemed grandfather, who raced clipper ships. I'm not sure I believe Rosenquist's insistence that he had no attachment to the various space and sea crafts in his paintings, these large fragments washed up upon the shore of his childhood imaginary—the flat land of North Dakota like a screen upon which one can project one's memories, as he has said—and I am suspicious of any claim, even by the artist himself, that his objects lack narrative or meaning, when one thinks of his father's work servicing B-24 bombers and other planes during the Second World War.

The following Monday, after taking a day to recover, exhausted and sore all over, possibly from a blocked milk duct, I call my father. We had missed our semi-regular Sunday call, as he was in the Ozarks with my brother and his children, seeing country-and-western revues and going to water parks, all of them un-masked as if there's not still a pandemic going on. Nice that you got on a plane to visit some grandchildren, I say to him, passive-aggressively, a jab he doesn't catch or chooses to ignore. I tell him about our trip to the seaport, and say I'd love to take him there when he visits in April, go to the museum, perhaps visit the Vietnam plaza, as there's no historical monument my father would refuse. Maybe, he says, in that noncommittal way of his. He won't speak about Vietnam; in fact, I never knew that he served two tours there during his career in the navy, on an aircraft car-rier that also recovered one of the Apollo missions, until his brother, his twin and also a navy man, told me as he was dying. Recently, for Veterans Day, my aunt sent me a series of photos of my father in his navy whites on a ship, for us to bring to my daughter's kindergarten, at her teacher's request. The children all drew my father pictures to thank him for his service, which we then mailed to him, including one child's drawing of a grave-yard, with the gravestones outlined in gray crayon. I've been to Battery Park, he now tells me over the phone, with your mother, in 1983, we went to Ellis Island as well. I ask him whether my mother, when she was visiting New York, probably for the first time since she left, wanted to visit the Bronx, where she was born. She said nothing about it, he says, but they did go to Glen Rock, New Jersey, to see the house where she spent her adoles-cence. Your mother was happy to see little children playing out-side in the yard, my father tells me. It is a house that should have children playing, she apparently said to him. Still, I wonder what this means, this strange omission of the apartment building in the Bronx where she was born and spent her youngest years. I look up the New Jersey address on Google Maps; it's a modest house, with daffodils in the front yard.

Did my mother research her family on Ellis Island as well? I ask my father, passionate genealogist of his own Italian American family. No, he says, it was only his family that they looked up. I bring up another old topic, wondering out loud whether we were Ukrainian Jews on my mother's side, and not Russian, and we have the usual conversation, where he accuses my maternal grandmother—whom I never knew, as she was alienated from her daughter after her divorce from her first marriage—of being a liar, as she always said she came over as a child from Moscow, which strikes him as impossible, as Moscow was not within the Pale of Russia, he keeps saying, the settlement where Jews were permitted to reside from the end of the eighteenth century until 1917. I tell him that I had long ago looked up the 1930 census, which came to my grandmother's home in the Bronx on April 2, the very date when I begin writing this essay, and that this confirmed that the family was listed as speaking Yiddish and being from Russia, all except thirteen-year-old Clara, my grandmother, who was born there in the Bronx, in the eleven-family tenement. My father responds by turning the conversation to Putin. Ironic, he says, complaining about the Nazification of Ukraine—the president of Ukraine is a Jew! The Russians, he grumbles, using thermobaric bombs. I say nothing to this, but all week I have been thinking, with a sensation approaching despair and horror, of the report that half of Ukrainian children have now been displaced. I can't erase from my mind that photograph, the following week, of girls and their mothers from Mariupol, Ukraine, at a shelter in Lviv, lying around, languishing—the Russians using hunger "as a weapon of war during the monthlong siege of the southern port," the caption reads. I keep thinking of this photograph, children my older daughter's age, one sitting there, ignoring a cup containing newly sharpened pencils, like those in Rosenquist's painting. The adults tried to read the children fairy tales, give them coloring books, all to distract them from their hunger. Something in that photograph reminds me, too, of Picasso's *Guernica*—the dead baby, the wailing mother, all in grisaille.

The phrase "women and children" reminds me of research I had been doing that Sunday after our walk around the extremes of downtown, wondering about the lighthouse we saw at the head of the Seaport Museum campus—a memorial, donated partially by the Vanderbilts, to the fifteen hundred people lost in the sinking of the RMS *Titanic*. The lighthouse was previously located on the roof of the Seamen's Church Institute at Coenties Slip, where it emitted a green light out into the Narrows for most of last century and dropped a time ball at noon, for the notice of all the residents and workers of Lower Manhattan and ships in the harbor—including my father, who remembers crossing the Narrows in a destroyer in the early 1960s. The Seaport Museum and its campus apparently saved by a massive corporation in return for developing one of those super-tall buildings that will mar the horizon, such as the monstrosity in Midtown that police had to cordon off this winter after it was determined that ice falling from such heights was threatening to impale pedestrians. We skirted the area one day as we walked to the Museum of Modern Art, where John was reviewing a show on the lower level. I stared with my daughters at Agnes Martin's gold grid painting entitled *Friendship*, whose expensive gold leaf was most likely paid for by money given to her by the weaver Lenore Tawney, who also titled Martin's paintings when she was in the hospital, in order to sell them—much to Martin's distress, as she was suspicious of language. (This distrust of titles she shared with Rosenquist, her successor on the third floor of 3-5 Coenties Slip, along with an interest in how to render metallic surfaces in painting.) After the museum, we took the girls to a playground in Central Park, where I watched my older daughter climb a tremendous rock, her father patiently trailing after her, before she threw a tantrum when we had to leave. Earlier that same February, I had watched my daughter and her friend, a few years older, play a game they called Titanic on a large playground structure in Fort Greene Park, after climbing up an immense gray rock together. Her older friend was leading the game, which my daughter played eagerly but I'm not sure she entirely grasped, as later she asked me whether anyone died on the *Titanic*. This was while driving on the West Side Highway on a Sunday in early April, heading toward Midtown, where we were going to see a loud and fairly traumatizing production of children's theater, our first show since the pandemic began. I had just pointed out Pier 59, the large, rusted structure stretching out into the Hudson where the RMS *Carpathia* brought in the *Titanic*'s few lifeboats carrying the remaining survivors, including two-month-old Millvina Dean, the last living survivor, who passed away not long ago in her nineties. The pier is a regular sight for us, across the street from the new Whitney, a gray-and-white structure like a massive washing machine, at the same address where Melville once worked as a customs officer. From that new building we recently peered out at David Hammons's ghostly three-dimensional line drawing, in steel, of another pier that stretches out into the Hudson. Directly behind Pier 59 is another futuristic park and playground of poured concrete, also meant to survive future storms, next to the monstrous sporting complex at Chelsea Piers. While driving there now I told John about the black-and-white photograph of crowds of anxious people waiting for the survivors, which I had researched earlier, and how freezing the children must have been, how long they had to wait.

As we drive farther down the West Side Highway we pass by the aircraft carrier *Intrepid*, docked on one of the piers. The ship, now a museum, is the exact type of carrier my father was on during Vietnam, before boarding the destroyer that deposited him at the Brooklyn Navy Yard in 1962. After arriving, he tells me over the phone, he saw a production of *Camelot* with tickets from the USO, although by then Julie Andrews had left for Hollywood. I try to imagine my father walking around Times Square in 1962, as he tells us he did: the screaming spectacle of the billboards, some of which James Rosenquist painted there in the late fifties, until he quit after two fellow painters he worked with died in a fall from scaffolding. Rosenquist later found inspiration for his collage compositions in the aggressive energy of billboards—a way to produce an effect of disorientation and numbness, he says in his memoir, that comes with the brutality of an enlarged image, his optical experiments in dislocation of scale creating images so massive that they overwhelm the viewer, familiar images so large in close-up that they become abstracted, in this way adapting the methods of a billboard painter, who created compositions meant to be recognized and comprehended only from far away, and which only billboard painters themselves usually saw up close. While serving in the navy, my father and his brother likely had to sit through an exam for colorblindness that was developed by the Japanese ophthalmologist and army surgeon Shinobu Ishihara, who hand-painted with watercolors the mosaics of dots that Rosenquist references so often in his mysterious compositions, playing on the optical illusions—the wit of the Ishihara colorblindness test here being rendered in grayscale. Thinking of Times Square in 1962, I find myself getting lost on the internet, reading that the area was once a forest with a beaver pond, back when Manhattan was the Lenape land called Manahatta, before the Dutch sailed through the Narrows. There were whales and porpoises in the Hudson then, and thinking of this I recall the lines from *Moby-Dick*: "How then is this? Are the green fields gone? What do they here?" Justin Barton speaking in *On Vanishing Land* of the process of abstracting out space to get to space. I wonder what my digressions are doing—are they going deeper, into the local, into space, or blurring or obscuring space?

Earlier in March, I lie on the gray concrete floor of the art storage facility, staring at the painting, my two daughters in the waiting area with their father, eating chocolate granola bars given to them by the receptionist, perhaps unwisely, melty chocolate in the hands of children on the immaculate blue velvet sofa. Later they come in. I like that the children can see what I am spending time thinking through, and so John and I can talk and think through it together later. Mandatory to see the painting in person, I was told, to get the sense of vastness, the immensity of scale, and I feel this, the proportion and effects of distance, all of these objects floating in space. The idea for the painting came from the area in space where the United States and Russia had jettisoned tons of space junk. "It occurred to me that this was a kind of permanent museum where nothing would ever disintegrate. Imagine an old square-rigged ship out there in fine shape, sailing on forever." Online I find the General Catalog of Artificial Space Objects, the most complete catalog of manmade objects floating in space, used rocket bodies and dead satellites, including even Elon Musk's Tesla Roadster. I think of the space junk of my consciousness, all of these floating images and objects and narratives. Exactly a year ago, trying to teach my daughter about the planets, I ordered a book on the solar system, a puzzle, magnets that still stick to our fridge. I spend time closer to the painting, the objects disappearing, the dotted effect, like space dust, the texture of the universe. The effect is something like darkness.

Later, John shows me Peter Juley's black-and-white photograph of a man and a woman in midcentury dress standing in front of Barnett Newman's large, dark painting *Cathedra*—standing up close to it, symmetrically on either side of the painting's white dividing line, one of the lines Newman called "zips." Newman's idea was for the viewer to stand close enough to commune with the painting, so that the line would appear only on one's periphery, a quasi-religious experience as distinct from the disorienting effect of Rosenquist, although both dealt with emptiness and the void. These figures in the photograph are looking at the painting as a billboard painter would, we realize. The other day I tried to explain the big bang to my daughter, in the bathtub, when she asked why the world existed, why anything existed. At the art storage facility I too stood next to the center of the painting, which felt like a black hole swallowing everything.

Earlier that day, as we drove to Newark, I told my daughter that I am trying to research black holes. They are, I think, frozen stars, which become powerful masses that pull things in space into them, absent of light. Perhaps later I will try to explain to her that if the Earth were compressed until it became a black hole, it would be smaller than a dime—but only if I can finally understand it. That space and time together form an infinite fabric, an outstretched blanket. That time is not straight but curved. That matter tells space-time how to curve, and curved space-time tells matter how to move.

THE WIND WAS FULL
OF SPRING

Saturday March 26, 2022

Begin here. It has just rained, a quick spasm, and somehow the grayness has turned to light, which floods the bedroom, and then flickers out again. The fragility of March here, this period of time the poet Francis Ponge called "the early-spring." How the weather changes so quickly. The dog is still hiding in the bathroom after the storm, disturbed by the boom of thunder, the sudden winds. I visit the raucousness in the kitchen, John dancing around, a child on each hip, while waiting for the pierogis and broccoli to cook for lunch. Watching their movement, feeling the transience, that brief moment of joy. Time as only an instant. I take a video, I'm not really sure why. When I come back, a minute later, the baby is on the floor dancing with a pink Care Bear that was around when we were children, and the five-year-old is eating applesauce out of the fridge with a fork. Now the sun comes in again. Something of the light during the afternoon now is both golden and gray. I struggle to describe it. I'm not even sure that it matters, whether or not I can describe it. Having any time and space to myself feels impossible lately. I yell out at my children to stop stomping around like elephants, so I can think. This breaks the spell. At least there is now silence.

The leaf blowers have stopped. The light comes out again, even brighter. The room glows.

I am in bed rereading the beginning pages of May Sarton's journal, which she kept when she was sixty years old, living in New Hampshire for a year, from 1970 to 1971. "Begin here," she writes on the opening date. I appreciate the directness of this, this command to herself, that it doesn't matter where she begins, simply that the journal must open on the day she's living. The journal is a space for her to recover herself and her solitude, after becoming burned out from publishing her work, from her communications with others. In the opening pages of the published journals, there is a black-and-white photograph of Sarton in her study, a vase of daffodils at her desk. Often these flowers, picked from her garden, function as a sort of still life for Sarton, an occasion to meditate upon the transience of life, amid despair and spiritual angst. In these opening pages, Sarton considers a spray of pink roses. Looking at this arrangement of flowers, considering their fragility, is a way for her to pay attention, to think about beauty, process, mortality, like a memento mori arrangement. (The English term "still life" is derived from the Dutch "stilleven," or "dead nature.") "When I am alone," she writes, "the flowers are really seen; I can pay attention to them. They are felt as presences. Without them, I would die. Why do I say that? Partly because they change before my eyes. They live and die in a few days; they keep me closely in touch with process, with growth, and also with dying. I am floated on their moments."

May Sarton's struggle with herself in this yearlong journal, and her attempt to live in the slow dailiness of her domestic space, appears to be a way to rid herself of the need for success and validation that she absorbed through her experience of publishing, and to attempt to face her interior life, in the space of a room. In some ways her circumscribed year of solitude in the New Hampshire farmhouse resembles that of Jean-Jacques Rousseau in his weeks of self-exile on a Swiss island, determined to free himself, as Sebald writes in his essay on Rousseau, of the "exigencies of literary production." In the walk he labels the Fifth Promenade, Rousseau locks away his books and ink and paper and devotes himself to the study of botany, a magnifying glass and a copy of *Systema Naturae* in hand, attempting to order and classify every grass, moss, lichen, and indigenous plant on the island, creating a flurry of lists, indices, and catalogues—still a form of intellectual labor, as Sebald ironically notes, not an actual relief from overwork. In her year of solitude—though, like Rousseau, she was not in total solitude—Sarton seems more at peace with trying not to write, even sometimes in her journal, but to find restoration in looking at the flowers. Here we get to the daffodils of her author photograph on January 18 (though they might well be another year's daffodils): "A strange empty day. I did not feel well, lay around, looked at daffodils against the white walls, and twice thought I must be having hallucinations because of their extraordinary scent that goes from room to room. I always forget how important the empty days are, how important it may be sometimes not to expect to produce anything, even a few lines in a journal."

The limit of my own ability to write lately has been writing to friends to ask what's growing in their gardens, as they often live elsewhere, many in houses or cottages. I also write in my journal about the flowers I have sighted, in this early New York spring, and to marvel at this cyclical feeling, which is both full and fleeting. In this way I think I'm working on—or perhaps not working on, for that is also writing—a notebook of seasons and exhaustions, a form I've termed "translucencies."

Time has become so vague and strange now. It's incredible to believe that two years have passed, or that it's been only two years, although my youngest is now eighteen months old, and I know I was pregnant when this all began, taking the same walks, in the same neighborhood, holding my older daughter's hand, walking the dog. The seasons are a relief in their repetition, the certainty of their return, especially the spring. Although spring always startles—to come out of winter, still in the gray and brown, and then begin to see clusters of color appear, as happens in an urban landscape, unplanned, unlike a formal garden. How reassuring to feel connected with Danielle in St. Louis, or Sofia in Virginia, as they report sightings of sneaky purple crocuses, the brightness of yellow forsythia. The purple comes, then the yellow, then the pink. It is in this period, of the opening, it is in this period, when it all began. The closures, with the opening. It's true, I remember.

This morning we all took a walk, in the grayness, noting as we do now the early signs of spring. I point out to the toddler the single, resilient Lenten rose plant in the garden out front, a garden

otherwise abandoned by our landlord, nothing else there blooming. There is trash everywhere, plastic bags and cups that have
floated in from the apartment building next door, that I keep
meaning to pick up. She puts one trembling finger to the dark
purple flower, the color of a bruise. I focus on that moment, of
her watching the flower. I think that, with this notebook I'm trying to keep, about paying attention to the natural world, I'm trying to come to terms with what Sofia calls the diminishment of
the world. The world as it is. An attempt to bring a reverence to
things as they are, to perceive the beauty of shabby things, and
also the shabbiness of beauty.

On our walk, which we still take daily, the same circumscribed
path, the two girls hold hands and stumble along the sidewalk,
picking up spiky brown brambles and sticks, while John and I
trail behind with the dog, watching them. The younger one is so
happy to be holding hands with her sister. I point out names of
flowering things. The yellow hyacinth in the church across the
street. The magnolia trees beginning to open. An aliveness in
the shooting-up of the green tulip stems. The funny assertive-
ness of the daffodil. First there was one daffodil, or two, and now
all of a sudden everywhere is yellow. Our destination for the
short walk, since it's slightly raining, is the large Queen Anne
house down the street that we love, whose elaborate garden has
been a balm for us, an infusion of beauty, especially since the
pandemic began. Let's walk to the garden, we say. Daffodils
everywhere. I marvel at the timing. Soon, I know, the tulips will
come, in syncopated blazes of color, in single rows in front of

houses, in monochromatic circles and crowding the flower beds in front of the mansions.

I think of the start of the pandemic, when we first had to pull my daughter out of preschool, and all we had was this circumscribed walk around our neighborhood. I was slow and nauseous, vomiting every day, everything was miserable. Then, all of a sudden, there were tulips we could walk to and see, keeping a safe distance from others on the sidewalk; we could go outside to the garden, to our garden, and see the rainbow display of the tulips. The feeling of this spectacle stirred a flamboyance in my heart. My favorites, the ones with flaring, flame-like streaks, which I learned, while idly researching tulips the other day—not writing, thinking about flowers—were the most extravagantly expensive bulbs during the Dutch tulip mania of the 1600s. These tulips, classified by primary color, Rosen, Violetten, the Bizarden ("the bizarre ones"), caused such a speculative bubble that one bulb came to be valued at the price of an expensive house. Later it emerged that these multicolored blooms, known as broken tulips, were the result of what was called a mosaic virus, caused by aphids. The broken tulips were smaller and weaker, and they made other tulips ill, but for this reason, somehow, they were more desirable. Some have argued that because of the immense loss of life suffered during the plague, which reached its height in 1636, many felt compelled to risk everything in pursuit of the flowers. The plague was a summer disease, and the height of tulip mania occurred during the winter of the next year. After being so exhausted by the years of plague, it seems the Dutch simply went mad for beauty.

Tulip Mania

In the early evening on this Saturday, I sit with my chin on our main table, my elbow resting on the mound of brightly colored children's clothes I have just folded and still need to put away. My love-hate relationship with the girls' laundry, which we do together, which is constant and never-ending. I am watching the two Covid tests on the table, watching the slight rose-colored line, willing another one not to form. Booger Popsicles, my daughter has taken to calling the tests. We have just received an email that there was a positive case in her classroom. As we wait—the result is negative, we finally see, probably because the children are still wearing masks—I watch the four wan purplish tulips in the jar on the dresser I have taken to calling the nature table, an effort I began this January to bring some brightness and color inside to fend off the winter gray. Although in the winters we merely stick twigs in the jar, we also arrange pinecones, wooden houses, and various peg people on silk scarves atop the table, changing the color of the scarves each month. For March I have taken to buying two bunches of tulips at the farmers' market every Sunday, putting them out with a plastic toy lion and lamb from the basket of animals, a visual pun my daughter doesn't yet catch. Usually we don't have a budget for flowers, but two bunches for ten dollars, even weekly, is not too great an extravagance. May Sarton writes of her desolation when there are no flowers in the house. Her feeling of ebullience with tulips in each room. The first time we got them, the tulips lasted for two weeks. This time, one bunch of orange blooms never opened, so I threw it into the overfull trash. The four purple flowers have taken up the empty space, stretching out in different directions in that graceful gesture tulips make, especially when they are fading, almost drained of color. There's beauty in a tulip that's near the end. In watching it wilt and stretch toward the light.

Two years ago, when my daughter's preschool came to an abrupt end and she was home all day, I had a desire, something approaching a mania, to teach her about the seasons. I think I believed that if I could teach her to celebrate the rhythms of the seasons, that would provide her with some stability, and something to celebrate as well. It would also be a way for us to divide time, which suddenly felt amorphous. From the blogs I read, kept by moms—all moms—who homeschooled according to Montessori methods, I gleaned that I could help her dissect a flower, something we could do together. I would put the dissected flower on a tray and label all the parts: the three petals and three sepals, the stamens, the stigma, the pollen, the bud, the stem. She was only three, and she wasn't very interested in the dissection, but she liked cutting up the flower. I did get her a few books about flowers, including one called *The Big Book of Blooms*, which she likes paging through. She talks about pollinators, because she's learned about them at kindergarten. I also got my nieces, who were older, these old-fashioned-looking flower presses, as if I were suddenly Emily Dickinson, tending to a Victorian herbarium. Lately I've thought of getting my daughter one too, as she is interested in nature, but I'm not sure whether she would use it. What would we do with all the pressed flowers? Stick them in books? I know they would scatter, sticky and flat, to the floor, where eventually I would sweep them up.

Thinking About Derek Jarman

For an hour or so one morning, I sit in my usual position on the couch, watching the children play out front with their father, as I open and start rereading the filmmaker Derek Jarman's gardening journal, which he began keeping on January 1, 1989, a few years after he was diagnosed with HIV. Online I also explore his sketchbooks, where he pasted photographs of his garden and pressed flowers. The beauty of Howard Sooley's photographs of Prospect Cottage, the tiny black fisherman's cottage where Jarman lived, with its yellow-trimmed windows, the wildness of poppies outside, a dotting of ornamental kale, the artist often posed next to one of his sculptures made from rusted flotsam washed up from the beach, wearing a coral jumpsuit. The cottage was located on a shingle shore in Dungeness, Kent, a desertlike terrain of "unruly sun" and wind, the other cottages and fishermen's boats seemingly abandoned. The eerie landscape has long been regarded as something like a postapocalyptic setting or mythic wasteland—not only for its location next to the brutal-looking nuclear power station Dungeness B, with its threat of nuclear accident, but also for the specter of AIDS, which at the time of Jarman's stay, in the absence of combination therapy, was a death sentence. A miniature steam train lingered in the distance, adding to the uncanny feeling of the scene.

At the beginning of his diary, Jarman describes the desolate landscape: the erosion of the sea leaving just a stony desert, the "flat ochre shingle," his only boundary the horizon. Such beauty in the language of his garden of wilderness, in what he has planted that day: "only the toughest grasses take a hold—paving the way for sage-green sea kale, blue bugloss, red poppy, yellow sedum." He planted on a very small budget, like his films, a spirit of radical grace and hope amid despair and relentlessness, doing this often intense labor even with a declining body, as he worried over the declining world, the ozone layer, climate change. The language of the diary is anachronistic, with an almost baroque tone. Upon observing the season's first crocus, he plants roses, an act that prompts him to a reverie of the romance of the nursery, antique-looking photos above each plant a brief botanical allusion to the old roses and their origins, sounding like a Victorian naturalist. The passionate recitation of the names of plants, "houseleeks and sedums, thrift, dianthus, saxifrage, campion, wallflower, purple iris, calendula, curry plant, rue, chamomile, columbine, shirley poppy, santolina and nasturtium." While planting rosemary, he makes allusions to Ophelia's bouquet. In this futuristic present, time is porous, slippery, and he writes with an elegiac gaze; his mind returns frequently to his peripatetic childhood in Italy, to his grandmother's garden. "But Gran's garden, in spite of its shadows, was a place of sunlight; no longer cultivated, its herbaceous borders long since softened by invading daisies and buttercups, it was slowly returning to the wild."

When he was four years old, Jarman recalls, he received a gift: an Edwardian garden book, replete with watercolors, called *Beautiful Flowers and How to Grow Them*. In February he counts fifty buds on the daffodils he planted the year before. They haven't opened yet, but if the warm weather continues they should open soon. A poetic reverie about daffodil bulbs, used by the Greek physician Galen, surgeon of gladiators, to glue together wounds and gashes, bemoaning how horticulture has destroyed the seasonal rhythms of daffodils and other varieties. To be a gardener, he writes, is to be in one's own time. I remember the gardening diary my mother kept, the only document I have of her handwriting, besides her calendar. How she struggled to continue it even as her health declined, so rapidly that she couldn't make it up the three stairs to the kitchen where it was kept. The last words she wrote were "Blue Hydrangea!!!" She was trying to keep her friend Emma's plant alive, she wrote, if she herself could survive the spring. I've already written about all this, in another book, but now, thinking of gardens and flowers, I think anew of my mother's perseverance. Something like optimism. She still cared about the fate of the plants.

I shouldn't say I "have" my mother's gardening journal, as I believe it is still at my father's house, where he still gardens, at least until this year, when he has had to hire someone to plant the geraniums and pansies that were my mother's favorites. He also continues keeping the gardening journal, writing brief notes about the weather and the progress of the flowers. My mother has now been gone nineteen years. The last time I spoke to my father, it was just after the anniversary of her death, in March.

That's what early spring is, always, for me. He tells me, as he does every year, that he has visited her grave. He won't plant flowers there yet, not until it's warmer, which he still does himself, crouching down, planting orange and yellow geraniums. He is able to do this because, he tells me later, he can pull himself up on her gravestone. Although in the past I've cringed at this ritual, probably because I find geraniums an ordinary flower, a symbol of the suburban lawns and small manicured gardens where I grew up, now I perceive the beauty of my father, now eighty-one years old, who in the past few years has survived a cancer scare and chemotherapy, along with several bad falls, crouching down to plant flowers at the grave of his wife, to whom he still feels married after almost two decades.

Later, on the phone, as I'm writing this, I ask my father about my mother's garden. She was never able to get spring flowers to grow, he tells me, and neither was he; he planted fifty daffodil bulbs last winter, but none of them took. I ask him about his father, whom I never met, as he died when my father was a young man, a sudden heart attack at fifty. His father kept a garden at the same house in Chicago where my aunt, who was seven when her father died, still lives. He grew geraniums and snapdragons, even roses, my father tells me. My uncle—my father's identical twin—grew pansies in the small back garden of that Oak Park house, and then my parents started growing pansies as well. Pansies. Pansies are for thoughts, Ophelia tells us. This is what I want to do. I want to think about flowers. I want to think about Derek Jarman thinking about flowers. I don't want to work. I want to see beauty as he does. "The rain and fine warm weather have quickened the landscape—brought the saturated spring colours early. The dead of winter is passed. Today Dungeness glowed under a pewter sky—shimmering emeralds, arsenic, sap, sage and verdigris greens washed bright, moss in little islands set off against pink pebbles, glowing yellow banks of gorse, the deep russet of dead bracken, and pale ochre of reeds in clumps set against the willow spinney—a deep burgundy, with silvery catkins and fans of ochre yellow stamens fringed with the slightest hint of lime green of newly burst leaves." There is even beauty in picking up the rubbish scattered over the shore, the glint of glass and pottery, military and fishing relics, which he then makes into towering rust-colored sculptures. The garden, like this journal, a bricolage. Beauty in the list of trash. "For two months after moving here I spent hours each day picking up fragments of countless smashed bottles, china plates, pieces of rusty metal. There was a bike, cooking pots, even an old bedstead." An arte povera, someone writes of the aesthetic of this landscape, an eeriness, after Mark Fisher's definition, that comes from being partially emptied of the human, yet everywhere haunted by its destructions.

Yesterday the Vale of Cashmere Where I Was First One Year Ago

Yesterday, after picking up our daughter from kindergarten, stopped in endless rush-hour traffic, we parked on Flatbush Avenue and entered an opening into Prospect Park, an opening into another era. We first stumbled upon this abandoned and seemingly private section of the park a year ago, while we were looking for a place where my father and his sister, making their long-awaited visit, could park easily and walk without having to climb any steps, and where there were bathrooms within walking distance, a list of criteria that this location failed. This visit would be my first time seeing my family, or my sister and her daughters, who lived upstate, since the baby was born eight months earlier—for the entirety of my pregnancy, for that matter. We didn't want to meet inside, despite their wishes, so we wound up finding a bench in the Long Meadow, with the late April sun surprisingly hot and bright, and the baby was passed back and forth on many laps. My father had recently suffered an injury of his optic nerve, after a bad fall; his eye was entirely bandaged, and he was wearing glasses that had the effect of magnifying the appearance of both his eyes. He seemed quite fragile; since then he's recovered somewhat, although I haven't seen him since his most recent fall. A distance has grown up between myself and my larger family, prompted by the impossibility of travel, from our point of view, and by their skepticism toward the public health crisis we've endured for the past two years.

The secluded enclave we stumbled upon, called the Vale of Cashmere, is a bowl-shaped area of the park, carved tens of thousands of years ago by the melting of the Wisconsin glacier. The park's architects, Frederick Law Olmsted and Calvert Vaux, initially included a small pool, gardens, and a children's playground, where children swung on parallel bars, sailed miniature boats, and played in the underbrush while their parents escaped from the sun and wind under the Rustic Arbor on the hillside. The name was granted by the wife of the Brooklyn mayor, inspired by a Thomas Moore poem titled *Lalla Rookh*, a romantic Orientalist tale set in the Mughal imperial court: "Who has not heard of the Vale of Cashmere / With its roses the brightest that earth ever gave." Eventually the topography was seen as inhospitable for a playground, and the Vale was turned into a "miniature Eden," a rococo landscape with exotic plants; downhill, the pool's soft edge was replaced with a Beaux Arts balustrade and a fountain, with two other round pools for water lilies. Among these was the Victoria Regia, a lily from the Amazon River basin, famous for its circular leaves enormous enough to hold a small child: one archival photograph shows a young girl in a white dress, her blond hair held up with a white bow like Alice of Wonderland's, sitting in the center of the flower, looking unnerved, while two women in formal Victorian wear watch from the benches, one in black as if in mourning.

Since then, the scene has become decayed and overgrown, the fountains variously dry or full of muck, the exotic plants removed. Because of its seclusion, the Vale has become a destination for migrating birds and for men looking for companionship. When we were first there, one year ago, as the baby drifted in and out of sleep on my arm, my older daughter ran around the three large stone basins that once held the rose gardens. I take a photo of the row of empty basins, the spookiness of the clouds, light shot through. Nearby, we find a structure made of sticks, with mirrors and strings of colored yarn inside—a fairy garden.

Similar structures dot the park, including a massive fort of sticks, large enough that my daughter plays inside. This year, emerging from winter, the empty stone pools are filled with muck and dirty rainwater; my daughters run around the sides while a few onlookers watch from benches. My daughter asks if she can play with the fallen logs that have come down after the recent heavy storm. I photograph a dead robin against the bright green grass, trying to record the strange lighting. There's something beautiful about this desolation, the red-brown of everything, as if the landscape itself is sepia-toned.

We walk down the steps to the former lily pond, also filled with muck, like on a ruined estate, patches of daffodils growing there stubbornly. The sounds of migrating birds. Two men with binoculars, who were speaking to each other when we first approached. My younger daughter is excited to see a lone male mallard in the mucky ponded rainwater. Duck, she says, pointing. The woods here were overgrown with weeds after a series of hurricanes, and many trees were damaged and felled. Goats were brought in to eat the poison ivy and honeysuckle vines on the steep terrain: a pair of Nubian brothers named Eyebrows and Horatio, an Alpine goat named Swiss Cheese, a Nigerian pygmy named Lily Belle. We wander over to what's called the Natural Exploration Area, built from the damaged and felled trees. My little one in her red-brown sweater and brown hand-me-down overalls, my older in maroon pants and a teal sweater, ambling together against a scorched landscape, wintry and brown. We watch them, remarking at the beauty of the landscape. "I have re-discovered my boredom here," Jarman writes in his garden journal, after quoting from Gaston Bachelard's *The Poetics of Space* on the open space of childhood. My daughters could be my sister and me as children, in our sweaters and corduroy bell-bottoms, their saturated tones. The baby holds a stick, scratches at the ground. She's framed by a great tree with a window cut out of it. One such door structure inside a tree has blown over, most likely from the heavy winds and nor'easters this March, possibly helped along by older children pushing it over. My older one walks across a log, jumps down. Climbs up to a ravaged tree trunk, sits in it like it's a throne.

We were here just last Sunday, for my daughter's friend's fifth birthday. All the children lined up to whack at a piñata. A flurry of parents sifted through the dirt, picking up candy wrappers, bits of string and sparkle. These few days later, walking the same ground, I spot the glints of colored trash, from birthday parties and picnics, threaded into the clover and grass. It will be there, probably, long after we are gone, this synthetic texture in an otherwise natural landscape.

When We Get Home We Watch Walden

I like that the original title of *Walden*, the film diary that Jonas Mekas shot with a Bolex 16mm over the course of four years in the late 1960s, was *Diaries Notes and Sketches*. I watch the film with a daughter perched on each side of me, John pulling up a chair to join us once he is done with the dishes. In an interview Mekas speaks of the difference between a written diary, which is retrospective, versus a filmed diary, where one must react, immediately, to ephemeral moments in time. There are many scenes shot in Central Park, so much like the park where we just were. The focus on the seasons. The intertitles feel like haiku: "In New York it was still winter. But the wind was full of spring." The sweep of camera in the forest, the brown winter trees, reminds me of the videos I keep taking of the girls in the park, or the close-up of clover on the ground. "I walked across the park. There was a fantastic feeling of spring in the air."

Babies and children are everywhere in Mekas's film diary. Groups of schoolchildren in the park. A family on the lawn. A close-up of a child having her hair brushed, which reminds me that the next day, Sunday, will be hair-washing day, a ritual for me and my older daughter, where I have to brush out the tangles in her long curly hair, which was chin-length at the start of the pandemic. "Suddenly it looked. Like spring." All the flowers in *Walden*. "Barbara's flower garden," with hands watering small flowers in a window planter. One, entitled "Flowers for Marie Menken," a swirly collage of close-ups of flowers, reminiscent of his mentor Marie Menken's own experiments with a handheld Bolex in the late 1950s, turning to cinematic collage after wanting her paintings to have more light and movement. The warbling in the five-minute *Glimpse of the Garden*, from 1957, reminds us of the ambient bird sounds at the Vale of Cashmere the day before; the panning shots of the Victorian garden suggest what might have once been there. How swiftly we move from shrubs to trees to pink-and-white flowers all over the garden, as if we are the birds, then deeper and closer to leaf and interior, as if they are just abstract forms. Finally we watch Menken's *Notebook*. "Raindrops," reads one cursive intertitle, the intimacy of the artist's hand. The privacy of such a garden setting, as if the flora is communing with itself, a dance with the camera like a visitation. A close-up of flowers trembling with slight rain, recalling the scene we just escaped on our walk, their vibrations. The swan swimming in a lake, much like the ones we see at Prospect Park in this late spring.

Lists of Flowering Trees

The close-up in Marie Menken's *Glimpse of the Garden* is of tiny pink flowers with fragile green dots. I believe they are flowering dogwood. I know this because, when my father visited again last spring, and we drove up to my sister's house in Westchester to see him, we spent some time discussing the flowering tree in my sister's backyard. It was April, so everything was flowering in New York. My father often took us to our local arboretum and botanical gardens growing up. The day before, on a visit to the zoo and the carousel, he had declared out loud the names of all the flowering trees. At my sister's, we couldn't figure out—or, I should say, couldn't agree on—what kind of flowering tree she had in her yard. Later, I looked it up: it was a flowering dogwood, a species unique to the East Coast. When I told my father this, he proceeded to look it up for himself, in one of his own flower books, as he later informed me in an email. It is always startling to me, to read my father's almost formal diction in an email, capitalizing adjectives and tree names as if he were an eighteenth-century essayist. You are right, Katie, he wrote to me. The Flowering Dogwood is an East Coast tree. We do not have them in Illinois. The Dogwood we have in Illinois is called an Uneven Leaf Dogwood. It does not have similar type flowers and leaves which is why I was Confused. We just call it a Dogwood which is also why I was Confused.

The lists that make up *The Pillow Book*, Sei Shōnagan's tenth-century journal of her life as a courtesan to the empress Teishi, record what she finds irritating, adorable, beautiful. She kept the lists to amuse herself as well as her fellow ladies-in-waiting, including her empress, who lived circumscribed and mostly interior lives, often behind a screen. Many of the lists come from observations of the natural world—of animals, insects, plants. The love that is in these lists. I come across one my father could have written: "Lists of flowering trees, flowering plants, waterfalls, rivers, bridges." Not only is she attuned to the absurdity of court life, but her diary entries and lists are imbued with a feeling of the seasons, that feeling of mono no aware, first documented during the Heian period, of sensitivity and exquisiteness toward the ephemeral, felt most profoundly during cherry blossom season. Cherry blossoms appear as vibrating forms within *The Pillow Book*—another list, of "Things That Lose by Being Painted," includes pinks, cherry blossoms, and yellow roses.

That spring, the second since the pandemic began, I relied on the extreme beauty of flowering trees, which we saw during regular visits to the park. The weekend before my father's visit, we went with friends, who had memberships, to the Brooklyn Botanic Garden, and visited the Cherry Esplanade in full bloom. The cherry blossoms were lurid, almost unreal, shot through with pink and purple. While the children played and the baby crawled over me, I lay down on the soft ground, the tiny pink petals as my bed, and watched the blossoms, like clouds overhead. How dark the sky, like a rainbow energy.

That month, my friend Bhanu writes me of how empty she feels in the caretaking vortex, after her mother suffered a period of illness. I replenish myself in nature, she tells me. I feel this as well, at the beginning of this spring, after the February of the children's fevers has exhausted me. Mrs. Dalloway wants to buy the flowers herself, after still feeling shaky from the Spanish flu. Yesterday I went to a bluebell wood, Bhanu writes me. The violet is still vibrating in my mind.

The Language of Flowers

My grandfather, who ran a butcher shop until he collapsed of a heart attack in his fifties, cultivated roses in his backyard— seventy-year-old roses that still grow there, long after he is gone.

Like Derek Jarman, he also planted a fig tree out back. Every year, my father tells me, he had to wrap it in burlap to protect it from the harsh Chicago winter. I watch a video of someone wrapping a fig tree, with a large unfurling of burlap; such attention and care, I think, to wrap a tree so that it survives winter. My grandfather, who likely worked himself to death but still kept up his hobbies, his gardening and photography. How he passed on to his children a love of the language of flowers, which my parents then passed on to me. The catalogue feeling of the many variations of botanic gardens I visited as a child.

Being outside with my father, in nature, is always how I felt the closest to him, the most in a quiet companionship. Every summer we go to the cabin that my grandfather helped build, in Michigan's Upper Peninsula, and take walks down the sandy trail with my father. I've been going there since I was a young child. Our trips to the cabin were my first real education in the deep solace of the forest. Picking daisies by the side of the road, gathering them in a glass at the windowsill for my mother. John has been going with me for the two decades we have been together—every year until that first pandemic summer. For years it was the two of us, and then the dog, taking slow hikes around the lake with my father. Now when we go up with him and my aunt, he also has two little granddaughters to ramble after him. It is through the language of flowers and birds that he connects most with them. Last summer, our older daughter brought her binoculars, and the bird book he'd bought her that Christmas. Her grandfather brought a book of Michigan wildflowers, and he would stoop with my oldest to look up the purple flowers growing at the side of the road.

In the essay "Reading Natural History in the Winter," Gillian Osborne publishes a list of flowers blooming and fading in a Boston garden on a particular day in October 1835. Beginning with the California poppy, she goes on to list asters in "many varieties, going off," pinks, several varieties of dahlias "in perfection," and on and on, for the length of an entire page. Such a list of flowers, she found, could be its own poetry, can be intensely moving—a feeling, she writes, that Emily Dickinson, also a lover of flowers, likens to the top of one's head coming off. There's something so excessive and voluptuous about lists of natural history. "That list, stuttering around perfection, of a half-dead garden on the other side of the country more than a century ago on the edge of a new season, gave me that feeling," Osborne writes. "Which made me realize: how barren and barely a thing was a poem." She thinks of her grandmother, who loved wildflowers so much that once, on a trip, she asked to stop so she could cup a flower in her hand by the side of the road. Osborne never knew much about her grandmother, she writes, except that she was a lover of nature, but she feels intensely moved by a list, which her grandmother wrote as she was dying, of the wildflowers she could see on the hill outside her window. In so many of these garden diaries I describe, there is beauty in the circumscribed, deeply observed life, in smallness.

I wanted to take the girls to the botanic gardens on Sunday, but it was too cold. Even though it is late March, it still flurried snowflakes outside of our window. That morning, instead, we walk to the farmers' market to get our bunches of tulips. Orange, pink, purple. We watch a woman outside the gated garden in the apartment building down the block strike the ground with an axe to break up the soil. Although I appreciate the choreographed gardens in front of the big houses, I also appreciate the flowers that reappear each year in humble or overgrown yards, solitary in their persistence. Magnolias, green tulip shoots, Lenten roses, everywhere, everywhere, the yellow branches of forsythia. The sole daffodil that shoots up, surrounded by dandelions. A new tree has flowered white in front of that apartment building; I make a note to look it up later.

MEDICI SLOT MACHINES

a series

sensitivity to tiny things

Our toddler is now at an age where she's likely to feel a sensitivity to Small Objects, or as I've also seen it phrased, an intense love for tiny things. Pieces of lint, scraps of paper, marbles. According to Maria Montessori, from birth until the age of six a child goes through many Sensitivity Periods, a transitory state where they are receptive to or passionate about certain activities. There are apparently eleven Sensitivity Periods, such as Movement (ages birth–1), Order (ages 2–4), Refinement of the Senses (ages 2–6), Writing (ages 3–4), Reading (ages 3–5). Sei Shōnagon speaks to this sensitivity to tiny things in *The Pillow Book*, which itself is a series of lists that are like a series of small objects. "Anything small is adorable," Shōnagon writes. For her this includes very small children, who crawl across her many lists of things—unless they cry loudly, which puts them in the category of the annoying or irritable. "When a child of two is crawling briskly along, it is adorable to see it alertly spot a tiny curl of dust, pick it up with its dainty fingers, and show it to an adult." This may explain why, as soon as my youngest began to crawl, her favorite game was to pick up lint from a particular woolen rug that we never had time to vacuum—and which has now been replaced by machine-washable rag rugs, which we still often don't clean, and are often stained—and proceed to put it in her mouth. She will put anything from the floor in her mouth, especially if it's small. Then we will have to wrestle it from her mouth. Every day, for many months, we remove these small collections of carpet pullings from her mouth and wipe them on the side table or the bookshelf. Sometimes they were composed of human hair, dog hair, bits of plastic, or the bits of baskets that we use to hold toys underneath every table or seat. While there is something sculptural about these wet assemblages, I doubt that Shōnagon or anyone else would find them adorable.

Often, when she is nursing, my daughter will take a bit of lint from my sweater, or from a blanket on the couch, and pop it in her mouth, then open her mouth wider and nurse. It's become a ritual for her. I don't know why my daughter needs to put lint in her mouth. Perhaps she finds the soft texture soothing. Anyway, she is beginning to do it less. Often now, when she finds a small bit of lint, instead of putting it in her mouth, she'll toddle over to the couch to show it to me. How strange that this gesture can repeat across centuries. As does the impulse to both observe and list these small objects, our own sensitivities.

marble run

The other day my daughter came home from kindergarten in a stormy mood. First her leggings got wet when she was playing outside, and the teacher wouldn't let her change. Then the boys wouldn't let her have a marble to use in playing with the wooden blocks of the marble run set. Their teacher keeps the marbles in a glass on a higher shelf. After a child has arranged a few blocks into a marble run, they are allowed to have a single marble to plop in, to watch and see if it follows the track they have anticipated. But my daughter complains that the marbles all get claimed by the older kids, the boys who so often seem to exclude her, much to her annoyance. Apparently, my daughter tells me, you are allowed to come to school with a marble, and it can be your own marble to play with, although that doesn't seem entirely in line with the communitarian spirit of the school. So the next day we let her go to school with her favorite marble, the only one we have that has a red, blue, and yellow swirl inside. She loves this marble, which also has a slight scratch on its otherwise smooth surface. I love it too. Is there anything more beautiful than a marble, which seems to contain a tiny universe?

For my daughter's birthday this fall, I asked my aunt and my father—I should really say my aunt, with my father's agreement—to purchase for my daughter a marble run like the one at school. The starter set of wooden blocks made in Switzerland was extremely expensive, as well as quite small, although for a while she was happy to sit with it at home, building a modest yet complicated maze. I have no idea how to put together the marble run set, and I'm amazed that my five-year-old can. It makes me so happy to watch her, totally absorbed in this puzzle. I feel the same way about the train set, and any other building toys, which I make sure she has, that I didn't have as a child. The marble run set now sits in a basket underneath the front console. Sometimes she will take it out and play with it, when she's in the mood, but she hasn't in a while. We never would have purchased it ourselves, but my father often wants to make a Big Gesture during the children's birthdays and Christmas. Like all the other wooden toys, like the Grimm's toys, apparently made with wood from a sustainable forest in Germany, it is one of those sets of blocks where you are eventually expected to acquire additional sets, gently coercing you into brand loyalty to this particular series of prohibitively expensive building toys.

The five marbles that came with the set, all of a single color, live in a sake glass with a panda on it, which we keep on the bookcase we use for their nicer toys, the wooden toys purchased mostly by their grandparents. The glass marbles clink distinctively when a child pulls one out, or plonks one back in. Marble, marble, the little one now begs, all through the day. Sometimes I let her play with one, when it's just the two of us, but only if I can really watch her. I try to remind myself that she's not trying to choke on a marble, she's exploring her world. Sometimes she rolls the marble on the ground, making a satisfied humming sound. Other times she will take a block from the marble run and plop it in the hole, observing where it goes. Then always she will pop the marble in her mouth, and if she does this too many times the game gets to be over.

The other day the blue marble rolled under the couch, and we spent time on the floor trying to find it, knowing that her older sister would be furious when she got home, as it's now her favorite marble, as the other one inevitably never returned from school. Sometimes I have the urge to get the children an entire bag of glass marbles, all their variations in color, how excited they would be. But also, when I think about it, I want an entire bag of marbles for myself. I want to roll these miniature worlds, these colorful forms, around in my palm and put them in a bowl, maybe a glass bowl, which I will somehow have to secure. I never have collected anything before, but the urge to collect childhood toys gives me a feeling that's not quite nostalgia, or at least not nostalgia for my own childhood. It is perhaps a longing for simple beauty. And a longing to give my children even temporary joy, which gives me joy. However, I do not get a bag of marbles. I know they would scatter everywhere. I know this because of what happens when my toddler begs for the very tiny primary-colored felt balls we keep in a tin on the shelf that are supposed to help her older sister learn how to trace numbers, on a wooden board that I purchased the year she was home, a fancy version of the Montessori tactile numbers, and which she's almost entirely uninterested in. Puff balls, the toddler says, pointing upward in such a plaintive way. She's starting to try to climb the bookcase, which is not affixed to the wall, in an attempt to get to these things that she loves. Sometimes—not often—I let her play with the miniature felt balls, which are also quite lovely, and after wrestling open the tin lid she inevitably scatters them everywhere. Even after I convince myself that I've found them all, I will be picking up an errant few for days. I'm trying to be aware of my daughters' Sensitivity for Tiny Things, but this also means that Tiny Things are littering my home constantly, at all times. I often don't have the psychic energy to pick them up anymore, or to clean up the floors at all. I either have to become more Sensitive or less Sensitive.

gifts

All of the colorful wooden toys at our front window, on the bookcase and underneath in baskets, were given as gifts, by far-away grandparents. It's the only section of the house I can manage to keep tidy, although with effort. The girls and their father have learned how to put these toys away on the shelves in the way I prefer, often in baskets made of natural materials, which I took pains to find. When I'm sitting at the couch I often look at the area in front of the window, with the light coming in, with some pleasure. This helps because the rest of the living area always looks completely trashed. Still, the toys on these two shelves are charming. The Grimm's stacking bowls, the stacking rainbow wooden arches, the blocks, the wooden bus, the wooden trees, the houses, the peg people. They make that corner beautiful, these painted wooden forms. Still, they are somewhat oppressive to me. I am aware that out of a desire for simple yet aesthetically attractive toys, a desire that not everything in the children's lives should be branded, this World of Wooden Toys becomes its own form of rampant consumerism. The toys are too expensive, but now we have them. I wonder sometimes if I am the one who is collecting them.

The grandparents on both sides expect me to come up with the gift ideas, and during a certain time of year I scan lists of the best Montessori or Waldorf toys for every stage of development. The negotiations with my aunt, especially, around birthdays and Christmas, back and forth over email, are constant. For my younger daughter's second birthday, at the end of the summer, I am half thinking of asking for a marble tree, although we do not have room. Their grandparents on the other side, whom they never see, like to buy all their presents from one particular toy shop here, as they can pay over the phone, and this shop carries a marble tree. There are so many different varieties of marble tree, sometimes known as a "small cascading ball tree," ranging from fairly expensive to extremely expensive. Like many of the girls' other toys, these are made in Germany. You drop the marble down the tree, the description says, and listen to it cascade down the rainbow wooden leaves, making musical twinkling noises. It would probably entertain them for an hour. I'm not sure where we'd put this marble tree. It is in no way necessary, although it is beautiful. Of course I'd rather have other, more practical gifts, like snowsuits and sweaters, or replacements for their constantly outgrown sneakers and boots, or help paying for preschool, but that is usually not a desired option, although I have pressed. It's not Gifty enough for them. I think they have to like the idea of a particular gift, to be able to picture the children playing with it. It helps if the toy reminds them somehow of their own child-hood. Perhaps the marble tree could take the place of the wooden ball tracker—a gift from my aunt and father for my daughter's first birthday—that's wedged between the front door and the bookshelf. A rope bowl of wooden balls, painted and plain, sits on the shelf within the toddler's reach, and sometimes she still does drop the balls into the ball tracker, to watch them kerplunk across and down, across and down. Mostly no one plays with it. The other day, I got an empty egg container from the recycling and dropped a wooden ball into each compartment. She took them out, one by one, and rolled them on the floor. Ball, she said. Her language is blooming. All words for domestic objects: "Oven mitt." "Cacker" for cracker. "Cado" for avocado, whose solid smooth pit, like a slimy, oblong version of one of her wooden balls, she likes to play with. During my older daughter's year at home, she and her father often tried to make their own ball runs, with the small wooden balls and stacked rainbows and blocks. There is a website I have spent too much time on, called Building with Rainbows, about how to set up a ball run using the Grimm's rainbows. Eventually I kept on acquiring more and more elements in order to do this, so fervent was my desire for them to keep engineering ball runs together—a basic building set, the semicircles and building boards.

The kind of play I'm describing recalls the white-painted cork balls that appear in so many of Joseph Cornell's box constructions, often suspended from above, balanced on paired metal rods, or with a metal ring nearby, suggesting some kind of run or game, and indeed Cornell let neighborhood children play with his boxes. His mother, Helen, had trained as a kindergarten teacher, and looking at Cornell's wood-framed shadow boxes, his grids and ramps, reminds me of the Froebel Gifts that he likely grew up playing with, toys designed by Friedrich Froebel, who in the 1840s invented the concept of kindergarten. Froebel

Gifts got their name because the materials were presented to the child, were treated as gifts, and also because they allowed adults to see the essential gifts in a child. In such a Gift the materials were all presented together, in a box to be opened, then put back together in the original form of the box, which was part of the play. There were six Gifts, a number that increased at some point to ten. Gift 1 contained colorful balls of yarn, to teach the child about form, movement, color. Gift 2 was two two-inch wooden cubes, one two-inch cylinder, and one two-inch sphere, a toy called "the children's delight" designed to teach the child about unity of forms, of these forms' relation to the rest of their environment, to help them develop a knowledge of shapes, and of forms of beauty (such as by spinning the solids, seeing their interconnectedness with each other, making sounds by tapping them together). Gift 3 was eight one-inch polished wooden cubes that came in a box. From there, the wooden building forms grew more and more complex. All modern blocks children play with today were inspired in some way by the blocks Froebel designed, and these early explorations in shape, form, and pattern also influenced modern art. Paul Klee, Josef Albers, and Le Corbusier all attended kindergarten. Frank Lloyd Wright's mother taught her son and neighborhood children in one of the first kindergartens in the United States, which she ran in her home. In his autobiography the architect credits the Froebel Gifts, mass-produced at that time by Milton Bradley, with teaching him about geometry and architecture, about the elegance of the grid, about the connection among nature, mathematics, and art. Buckminster Fuller, known for his geodesic domes made of triangles, has said he built his first space-frame structure at kindergarten, by connecting Froebel peas and sticks (nodes and rods).

On my first visit to a Montessori classroom, I was taken by how beautiful and ordered everything was. There was harmony in how everything was arranged. The wooden shelves—holding puzzle maps, movable alphabets, and other materials designed by Maria Montessori herself—were meant to enable a child to take the toys out to play with and to figure out by themselves how they worked. Montessori's tablets and cubes were also inspired by Froebel. The beauty of the toys allowed for a calm, aesthetically appealing environment, to allow creativity and play. I felt the same way when I first entered a Reggio Emilia classroom or my daughter's Waldorf kindergarten. Rudolf Steiner also designed classrooms, desiring an organic and tactile feel to the spaces, the painted walls in the ascendant classrooms differentiated by Goethe's Theory of Colors, the built environment as spiritual exercises in harmony and geometry. As in my daughter's classroom, at home we have a Pikler triangle, the small climbing structure named after the Hungarian pediatrician Emmi Pikler. All of these early childhood experts were also designers. They designed toys and furniture, even the paint on the walls, because they believed that children play and learn best in beautiful, calm, light-filled, open environments. In the time before, when I had my child at home, I wanted, despite all our clutter and lack of space, to make my living area such an environment.

For the baby's first year, I searched for Montessori toys to help with movement, fine motor skills, and stimulation, but it was impossible to get everything, as there were so many frequent changes of development. The baby would roll a little wooden toy across the floor, and a month later you would have to get a longer version of that same wooden toy. I did get many wooden toys, some from IKEA, some handmade, to stimulate the baby and encourage movement during tummy time and afterward—the rolling ball cylinder, the rainbow spinning drum with the flashing mirror that made the satisfying clank from the marble inside, the soft balls in a bowl, the three-shape puzzle, the object permanence box with ball tray, several stages of ring stackers, the shape sorter, the wooden egg-in-cup and peg-in-cup or interlocking discs for fine motor skills. I tried to make some myself, following instructions from the Montessori blogs, like the magic tissue box made with a bamboo tissue holder and felt squares cut in one corner with a slit so they could be interconnected. It's hard to marry what has become for me a genuine interest in childhood development and education, as well as an appreciation for these toys, with the resulting consumerism perpetuated by these home-schooling blogs, which are at once a service and also a shill. The labor continues to be entirely maternal, exacerbated by the pandemic—and in the United States it was almost entirely women who disseminated Froebel's thinking, running kindergartens often out of their home. It's all so costly and confusing, this desire to have these toys at home. There are too many variations. All these progressive philosophies of education, with their intersecting design philosophies, have proliferated different sets and toys sold in countless Etsy shops, bespoke children's boutiques, month-long subscription series. I long for the simplicity of getting just one set of the Froebel Gifts, which were sold in the general store in the Swiss city of Bern run by Robert Walser's parents, as I read in Susan Bernofsky's biography of the writer. Since reading this, I like thinking of Walser's paragraphs of prose as conjuring the "bright open nursery" he remembers from his childhood in *The Tanners*. Also a passage like a gift, a box meant to be opened, filled with forms and shapes.

I've mostly stopped searching for wooden toys for my children. I'm not sure exactly why. I feel they have enough. We already have so many toys they don't use. I'm also just exhausted.

soap bubble set

"Moon" and "bubble" are my daughter's favorite words. Moon moon moon, she babbles around the house, from a song about the moon. Moon night, she says, pointing to the moon in a book. "Bubble" is her word for any small container holding water. She is also obsessed with catching bubbles we blow for her, in a yellow plastic wand, one of many iterations from the dollar store near our small local playground. Bubble bubble, she will beg. We have to guess whether she means a bottle of water or actual bubbles. In many of Joseph Cornell's soap bubble sets, the white ball is either a moon or a bubble, or perhaps both, and it seems to rise out of a pipe, one of the Dutch clay pipes he acquired from the Netherlands Pavilion at the New York World's Fair. The boxes often archive his vast collection of children's toys, most likely acquired later but remembered from his own childhood, like the blue marbles that rest in the bottom of plastic cordial glasses in the soap bubble sets, which were his first boxes.

Cornell's iconography of soap bubbles was inspired by a public series of lectures for children called *Soap-bubbles: Their Colours and the Forces Which Mould Them*, by the British physicist Sir

Charles Vernon Boys. It makes sense that Cornell, whose final two exhibits from his lifetime were for children, would be interested in a Victorian series of lectures for children on the properties of soap films. "I do not suppose that there is any one in this room who has not occasionally blown a common soap-bubble, and while admiring the perfection of its form, and the marvellous brilliancy of its colours, wondered how it is that such a magnificent object can be so easily produced," Boys writes. The frontispiece of Boys's text is the sentimental painting *Bubbles*, by John Everett Millais, which was disseminated widely as part of an advertisement for soap. The picture is of a cherubic child with soft blond curls, in a velvety costume with a white collar, holding a clay pipe, staring up at a bubble that the child has produced in a bowl. The child was Millais's five-year-old grandson, apparently, but the artist modeled the painting after a seventeenth-century Dutch vanitas, in which young boys were often depicted blowing bubbles, a meditation on the transience of youth and beauty.

A recurring presence for the more extravagant summer birthday parties and other celebrations in Prospect Park is Bubble Dad. Bubble Dad has outfitted himself with a set of bubble-producing devices of his own design, including a woven contraption, composed of a bit of netting suspended from two poles, that produces a cascade of bubbles in varying sizes, as he lectures on the physical and chemical properties of bubbles. In some ways, C. V. Boys was the original Bubble Dad. Apparently, he would often prank passersby outside his office window by blowing out perfect bubbles or smoke rings in order to entrap them. Likewise, in Bubble

Dad's finale, he surrounds each willing child within a giant bubble of his making. Last summer, my then four-year-old was too nervous to be trapped inside a bubble. At the end of this party, for the requisite gift bag that often contains candy and some sort of disposable souvenir, the host mom gave each child a clay pot with a yellow seed-ball inside, a ball that reminded me of the yellow balls in one of Cornell's soap bubble sets, and also of the sun. I think too of the yellow sand he used inside his sand fountains, which he got from pet supply stores, and of the two pots that appear in Millais's painting, originally titled *A Child's World*: one broken, the other growing a new plant—a memento mori.

On the opening pages of the philosopher Peter Sloterdijk's first book of his trilogy of spheres, *Bubbles*, he performs a close reading of the Millais bubble painting, in language that itself seems Victorian, almost conjuring the same sentimental melancholy: "Now a swarm of bubbles erupts upwards, as chaotically vivacious as a throw of shimmering blue marbles." The bubble is an "iridescent object," a "nervous entity," which holds a child's fascination until it drifts into the air into nothingness. The orb holds the attention of the child during the duration of its life, which is temporary. The blower has a sense of solidarity with the bubble, which excludes the rest of the world. In his treatise on spatial and architectural communities and interiors (placentas, domes, apartments, and so on), Sloterdijk is thinking through isolation and togetherness, working toward a general theory of communal atmosphere and climate change, of sharing breath and air as well as immune systems, even more relevant now, as we've come to speak of ourselves as living in "bubbles," having a "pod."

I think Sloterdijk is ultimately writing of a desire for solidarity and community, for "shared vibrations." But I also like thinking of bubbles as bubbles. The bubble is a form of the ephemeral, much like childhood itself. We all once had childhoods, we all once blew bubbles, and all of that has now floated away.

medici slot machines one

I've been thinking of how the Victorians aestheticized children this way, as in the Millais painting, their innocence and beauty—idealized narrowly within a certain class, white and wealthy—and whether these ideas still influence how young children are photographed. Not long ago I exchanged texts with a poet I admire but don't know very well, who also teaches at the university, though unlike me she is full time. She has a daughter one year older than mine, and just before the pandemic began we were trying to plan a playdate. Later, she also had a private pandemic baby, whom she also named after a male poet. When I texted her congratulations, she sent back a photograph of her five-month-old baby sitting on the bed, gorgeous in the sunlight, wearing tights and a bodysuit with a ruffle collar. There's something so noble and mournful about a baby in a ruffle.

When I had my first, I dressed her sometimes this way, in tights and dresses like a nineteenth-century child. Now I usually just dress the toddler in hand-me-downs, mostly oversize tees and leggings or shorts drooping at her knees. Most of the time she looks like a feral wrestler—gunk on her face, bangs always in her eyes. But I answered the poet's text with a photograph I had taken on my phone of the two girls in pajamas, on the bed, cradling each other, the sunlight coming in through the window, each of them holding a doll. Sometimes I wonder if there's something wrong, or unbearably nostalgic or sentimental, about these beautiful photographs of our children, that we text each other privately through the pandemic. There's the fiction within the photograph, its light and beauty. All last winter, in the period I think of as the abyss, I would stage the baby naked on a blanket, as she was doing tummy time, with that perfect cleave of baby butt, with her mirror and her rainbow-colored drum, that when turned would flash the mirror and clank a marble inside. I sent the photographs out to friends and my father. She's not crawling yet? my father would answer skeptically. They had still never met, would not meet until that Easter. He grew wistful hearing that she'd learned to sit up. She's not even five months, I told him. That was the period when she was peak Renaissance Christ baby—an exquisitely tiny person, with rose-gold curls and blue eyes, with the sweaty milky folds of her body. At six months she would sign to us, making her little fist open and shut, milky, milky, milky, an action she would repeat while holding and squeezing a hard-boiled egg in her hand. After every nap she seemed to have grown.

My father insisted on a portrait of each of his baby granddaughters at the age of nine months—only the girls, which annoyed me. These he hung on the ancestral portrait wall upstairs in his house, next to a tinted photograph that was apparently my mother at the same age, with her hair and dress tinted yellow, and her eyes blue—a touch that always struck me as artificial, as my mother's were dark like mine. Nine months: the age of absolute babyness. He wanted to take the photograph himself, on his small digital camera that he often fumbles with, around Easter, when they came for their first visit since the pandemic. For months I was annoyed by my sister-in-law as well as my sister (always this feminine labor), repeatedly checking in to make sure we were planning to take the photograph. He even paid for an Easter dress for the baby, as he was annoyed that my first wore a romper in her portrait, which we took awkwardly against the blank wall of a hair salon, as we didn't have a blank wall in our dark and cramped space. When they visited for Easter Sunday, out back on our patio, everyone took so many photographs of the baby with their phones to make sure they got a shot. She was instantly whisked onto her grandfather's lap, which she minded less than she did this past Easter, when she cried and begged off. And yet we got the shot, of the baby, at pure baby, staring at the camera with something like curiosity.

medici slot machines two

In one of the artworks he called his *Medici Slot Machines*, Joseph Cornell featured a reproduction of a portrait of Bia de' Medici, the "natural," or illegitimate, child of Cosimo I, who is said to have been forced by his new wife to send the girl away to live with her grandmother, until the child died suddenly of a fever at the age of five. The portrait was commissioned after her death—not as an official state portrait, but to be hung in the family's private rooms as a memory of the child, the internet tells me. This form of portraiture often happened with the Medici aristocratic children raised away from their family; a miniature might be commissioned, for instance, to be worn in a locket. There's a link here to the photographs of young children taken during a pandemic, away from more distant relatives, children who in many ways had disappeared by the time they reconnected, having grown older, in some cases out of their baby and toddler years altogether.

In Cornell's box the portrait, by Bronzino, is tinted with the artist's melancholy blue—blue-aille, as he called it—while the smaller compartments are filled with fragments of her face or hands, along with images of miniature unicorns as well as small blocks. In another of the *Medici Slot Machines*, Cornell features a portrait of nine-year-old Massimiliano Il Stampa painted by Sofonisba Anguissola, wearing a severe ruffled collar matching his severe expression; in boxes below the portrait are jacks, a red marble, and a compass. The way these children are posed, replicated in series of miniatures in the cabinet slots, reminds me of the class photographs we were sent this fall, just before my daughter's fifth birthday. The photographer had instructed her on how to pose, she told us, pantomiming to our approving laughter—first to one side, then to the other, then jumping up in the air, then finally facing forward, grinning widely, as if she'd been asked to hold her grin. Faraway family ordered prints of the photographs, to our bemusement. We didn't order any of these class portraits, preferring instead more natural, candid snapshots of our daughter looking like the stringy-haired bassist of a 1990s post-punk trio, glaring at the camera.

What to think of this preference, for the posed child? My grandmother's house was filled with black-and-white portraits of my aunt, my father, and his twin brother, my uncle, as children. Everywhere on the walls in my home growing up were the historical scowls of solemn children waiting for their picture to be completed, or the wide rehearsed smiles of me and my siblings. My mother would spread out the tiny squares of our class portraits across the kitchen counter, to see how we'd grown over the years. The names of the photo studios often are found printed across the front; my mother collected these sample prints, sometimes even framing them, rather than place an order for unmarked prints. I think of these photos when I read how, after Peter Hujar died, David Wojnarowicz spread all his childhood photographs out across his bed, the bed that was Hujar's before him, and asked how any mother could not have loved this boy.

In the mythical Winter Garden photograph at the center of Roland Barthes's book *Camera Lucida*, his mother, Henriette Barthes, was five years old, and having her portrait taken with her older brother. In *Camera Lucida*, the son regards his mother as a child, and finds something like her essential innocence in that photograph. Joseph Cornell considered children to be sovereign, or royal, believed that there was nothing nobler than a child. Perhaps, critics suggest, the morbid, sentimental glaze of his Medici boxes reminded him of his own more bourgeois childhood, in the family's house in Nyack, before his father died. I think of that photograph of Cornell and his sister as children, in a wagon in their gated backyard, in ornate, flouncy white Victorian dress and extremely floppy hats. Of his desire to collect these children, just that way.

object

The first winter I spent trying to homeschool my daughter, I became convinced that she needed to work on stringing beads. On
the Montessori blog I often frequented, the writer documents her
four-year-old's free-form embroidery, involving sewing tiny
glass beads on a burlap-covered hoop after school. Or perhaps
this was her daughter years earlier, as I believe she recycled content. See how calm she looks, sitting at her little table, stringing
beads. I wanted that for my daughter, that calmness and attention. I bought a sack of pony beads online, along with a spool of
rainbow string, and presented it to my eldest daughter on a tray,
with the pony beads placed in an empty jam jar. I got yards of
burlap, with its fibrous, slightly pungent smell, as well as embroidery hoops, and big plastic sewing needles. She liked stringing the beads, making necklaces and bracelets, especially that
summer, but she wasn't interested in embroidery. The pony
beads sat in the jam jar on a shelf above her desk.

What is a pony bead? asked the receptionist at the pediatric urgent care the following January, when my daughter was home

again, a week after winter break, because of the new variant. They couldn't see the bead, a light-blue pony bead, which she had suddenly crammed deep into one nostril that Sunday morning, as she was playing in her room after our walk to the farmers' market, when she had to be quiet while the baby was napping. Realizing what she'd done, she had confessed to me immediately. How a day can totally disappear in an emergency. Hoping to avoid going to a pediatric urgent care or ER, we spent six hours trying to extract the bead from her nose, which we couldn't see, but could feel—all while trying to keep her calm, as her bouts of panic were punctuated with our breakdowns as well. We tried almost every tip we found online, except Krazy Glue on a stick, which we were too nervous to attempt. We asked her to blow hard into a tissue; we tried to suction the bead out with the Nose Frida, a tool we used for clearing the baby's clogged nose; we attempted to pry it out with a device from Duane Reade designed for removing blackheads. We knew to try "mother's kiss," a technique the pediatric urgent care made me repeat as well, my mouth attempting a suction through my daughter's dry and chapped lips, blowing in repeatedly while plugging up her left nostril, hoping the pressure of my breath would expel the bead. We tried using a neti pot to irrigate it out, and she screamed in the bathtub like she was being waterboarded. At one point the shower curtain tension rod crashed down on both of us. Hours later, when we finally did have to go to pediatric urgent care, the doctor used a hook just like the one we purchased at the drugstore, but she succeeded in removing the bead, while the nurse and I held my daughter down.

Later, I had a vague memory of cramming a jack in my nose as a child, and my mother using pepper to get me to sneeze it out. But something made me wonder if this had really happened to me, or if I was somehow experiencing my sister's childhood memory on my body, as can sometimes happen. My sister confirmed that it happened to her when she was five, and I would have been four. I ask my father if he remembers; he seems never to remember anything about our childhood, although he can recall the smallest details of his own. No, she must have been only three or so when that happened, he now says to me, questioning his child's own memory, not his own. So why does it feel like my memory? I ask him. Because you were there, he says. Your mother had to take you to the pediatrician's office. All three of you. I only found out when I came home. Your mother didn't even call me. She was so apologetic, he says. Why? he asked her, you have nothing to apologize for.

I try to picture all this, to viscerally imagine my mother this way, tearful and apologetic. How chaotic one five-year-old can get. It rattles me when mine makes noise when her baby sister's napping, or jumps on me with full force, or is generally playfully insane, not listening, bouncing on the couch. Three children around the same age, her husband away at the office, she doesn't feel she should bother him. Was my mother furious when my sister put the jack up her nose? As I'm thinking this, still talking to my father, an ad pops up for jacks, with a rubber ball. But you want to hear a really funny story? he says. He proceeds to tell me how my aunt, his much younger sister, swallowed a safety pin as a baby. She was only eighteen months old when it happened, he says, but she knew enough to tell her mother that it was closed when she swallowed it. Your grandmother and great-grandmother had to watch her stool, he tells me. Of course it was the women who had to, I want to say. Always so clear, these narratives of his own childhood. Perhaps because he was there? But inevitably comes the jab—this is the funnier story—and the boast, that my aunt, the medievalist, was fully talking at eighteen months old.

wonder cabinet

The toddler runs to her sister's desk, climbs onto the chair and then the desk—a translucent console that once held plants in the front room, and later library books somewhere else, in a long-ago iteration of this apartment. On her shelves, my daughter has arranged something like a Wunderkammer, a collection of wondrous and curious objects, that are supposed to be out of her little sister's reach. I make a catalogue of these changing shelves in my head, her own groupings and gatherings. A painted green box from summer camp that holds a dead cicada, with its iridescent wings, as well as shells and other small objects—plastic insects, coins, marbles. A wooden mushroom that offers a kaleidoscopic insect-vision when peered through, from an old subscription box. A crystal. A knitted miniature pouch necklace from a school fair. Tiny sculptures she's made of beeswax: little animals and plants, tiny red berries for the January nature table. A small wooden box with a clasp, full of tiny miniatures—once her set of language objects, now just toys she plays with. The small heart-shaped cactus I got her for Valentine's Day this year, in its pot on the edge of the highest shelf, near the slim east-facing window. The painted mason jar for the lantern festival, with the gray felt bunny hidden inside that she got from her teacher for her birthday this year. A pink embroidered bag with a zipper, a gift from Sofia the last time we saw her before the pandemic, a bag that used to hold knit finger puppets, and now holds even more small objects.

The last time I looked at my daughter's shelf, everything was blue: a blue glass rock, a blue rubber ball, and my high school class ring, with its blue stone, which she is convinced is very valuable. Until recently, this was located in a plastic baggie full of jewelry, my mother's and my own, which I found amid batteries, masks, old phones, expired passports while cleaning out our junk drawer. A small leather pencil case that was a birthday present from one of her school friends, which now holds foreign currency I gave her as I was sorting through the gallon bags of coins her father had hidden in the closet—bags that still languish behind the couch, although I'd had all sorts of plans for the hundred dollars we'd collect when we put it through a coin-counting machine. My uncle used to collect foreign coins like the ones in my daughter's pencil case; he would give them to us as special keepsakes—always precious items to me, coins from other countries, as I had never been on a plane. My daughter likes to spread tokens out across her shelves, sometimes also on her desk and dresser, and there they are, until I try to clean them up or put them away. She's also afraid, rightly, that her sister will get them.

A happy-meal plastic dog that wags its tail when you click the wheel underneath. A bracelet of pony beads and a painted-shell necklace, birthday gifts from friends. A tiny toy car. A big swirly glittery pom-pom. A tiny plastic unicorn from some long-ago party bag. The toddler's favorite activity is to go through the painted red paper sleeve full of valentines her sister's class (or mostly their parents) had made for her on the day she had to miss because she had strep. There's one particular valentine, a tiny red heart on a Popsicle stick, that the toddler loves to take out and play with. Seeing it, I think of Ray Johnson's artwork *Valentine for Joseph Cornell*, a pink heart on which is pasted a cardboard collage, and of Cornell's own dovecote cabinets, in which he placed pink and red rubber balls, tiny blocks, a miniature gold vial. The crinkle of pink metallic candy wrapper in one of the vials like miniature apothecaries. I think also of the candy wrappers from the small chocolates stuffed into colored plastic eggs that my aunt and father gave the girls in their Easter baskets. Along with these, two tiny felt Easter babies I picked out, which they cooed over at first sight, and which now live on the spring nature table, on the top shelf of a small repurposed bookcase. The toddler has already bitten off the tiny ears on hers, although it still works as a tiny felt fairy baby. The plastic eggs I surreptitiously threw out after a few weeks, as they lived in their baskets on their dresser, untouched except when the toddler took each one apart and then dropped each half onto the floor.

magic box

For two years I've rearranged on various Word documents a list
of the items in David Wojnarowicz's Magic Box, the collection he
kept under his bed of fifty-nine small objects, stored in a wooden
citrus pine box whose sliding lid was labeled "Magic Box" on a
strip of masking tape, in marker, in his hand. I keep thinking of
the artist's box practice, much like Cornell's, as well as my daughter's collecting. There's a resonance I haven't been able to entirely
figure out. In his Magic Box, Wojnarowicz collected what children collect, or possibly this is an actual collection kept from
childhood, or recollected, like Cornell, by seeking out nostalgic
items from his childhood after becoming an adult. Wojnarowicz's
collection also included a fair amount of religious kitsch, as well
as a host of travel souvenirs. Also catalogued in Objects and
Artifacts in the Fales archive is an extensive collection of masks,
dolls, animal figurines, globes, the kinds of objects incorporated
into his videos and paintings. I've sometimes wondered, as have
others, whether the box is in fact Peter Hujar's, because of some
of the items (the crystals, the prayer cards), or whether Wojnarowicz incorporated these magical items into his own collection, in
an elegiac way, after Hujar's death.

My daughter and I often sit together and look at photos from the Magic Box, as recorded in the library's finding aid, a guide to the contents of an archival collection. I feel she understands it even more than I do. Maybe there is something to this, that to be an artist is to be close to childhood. The Magic Box holds a bag of plastic insects and bugs like the ones my five-year-old has, and other items resemble her collections: animal figurines, a collection of foreign coins, stones, glass, and crystals arranged by color, dried flowers, beaded necklaces, all housed in various smaller containers, like embroidered purses and plastic bags. There is magic to the list, to the actual fragments on the page. I keep thinking of all the hands that have held these items, that have catalogued them, either for the library or for their own personal notebooks and research. I keep copying the list into various documents, keeping them with me, adding my own descriptions based on the images. The list becomes its own collection, some magical coded privacy that is somehow communal. The list is its own poem.

Unopened bag of plastic insects and bugs

Green and white cloth stuffed snake with embroidered dots of red and purple

Yves Klein blue small painted animal skull

Tin snap toy alligator with feather attached to its mouth

Wooden crucifix with circular shell inlays, green tin Jesus

Japanese toy watch with green felt strap and red face
(does not work, time set to 10:30 Saturday 25)

Yellow and hot pink action figure with smoked-out face,
movable joints

Red plastic oval Catholic prayer piece

Two miniature globes, one that is a pencil sharpener

Green rubber grasshopper

Tall bright blue prayer candle, with white, red, green,
orange rings

Italian male wooden religious statue

Plastic snowman ornament with glitter

Small Buddha statue

Turquoise embroidered purse

Leather bracelet rimmed with red stones

Japanese dog-headed toy

Turquoise embroidered snap purse from New Orleans

Framed photo of a young yogi

A smaller cardboard box containing: postcards, joker card,
red stone in bag, another bag of three turquoise beads, bag
of buttons made from Indian-head U.S. coins, large
turquoise and brown beads in bag, small fossil insect,

cream-colored rock, teardrop red gem, metal sphere, quartz stone

Small carved animal, maybe a frog

Essential oil bottles with gold screw tops in bag, labeled Ants in Amber

Chunk of concrete with blue paint, looks like a crystal

Envelope of paper foreign currency, including Argentine pesos and Turkish and Israeli bills

Tiny framed black and white photo of a man, with a metallic green border

Dried flowers in empty plastic audio cassette tape case

Little cardboard box lined with green stuffing of charms and pins, metal and bone or ivory, including a metal pin of an antlered deer with a cross on its head

Bag of various shades of green and blue stones and glass

Large clear quartz stone wrapped in tissue paper

Four stones (possibly quartz): one large pink, one purple; one clear; one clear quartz embedded in gray stone. All wrapped in tissue paper

Collection of knives and tweezers—Buck Rogers Space Ship knife from early 1950s

Three toy metal trains

Plastic bag of seven polished red and brown stones

Another clear quartz

A clustering called a group of figurines: flag rubber stamp
and box of razor blades, including two plastic cowboys,
one a bright red, a ceramic green alligator, alien figurine
with a plastic shooter, black and green plastic fly

Gathering of brown, pink, and orange stones

Gray molded face pin with pink triangle carved and
painted on forehead

Plastic box of dried flowers, feathers, tiny shells, stones

Box of four rings, one dark metal with dragon design and
large turquoise stone, one gold-colored with a dinosaur
image in black and yellow

Bag of gold metal Kachina charms

Bag of seeds

Bag of charms and chains: Two silver necklace chains, one
silver bracelet. One silver bracelet with charms. Loose
silver charms: four smiling skull charms; cow, windmill,
raccoon, chicken, elephant, elk, giraffe, kangaroo,
jackalope, boar, swinging monkey, tiger, fly, bag of
money, crawling baby, pair of dice, handgun, clown, hand
in handcuff, anchor, sphinx, man wrapped around
lamppost, hut and palm tree, truck, ship, aircraft carrier,
St. Hubert medallion, Mickey Mouse, Minnie Mouse,
Donald Duck, Goofy, three See No Evil monkeys in bag.

Loose silver charm tags: two New York World's Fair
flags, New York flag, New Mexico, Trees of Mystery,
Grand Canyon, Colorado. Copper kneeling man charm.
Three empty gun shells. Flattened coin. Blank paper tag.
Silver jewelry ring. Earring ear wire.

Two gray stones with interesting white marks

Glass vial with porcupine quills

Two metal charms, one of a meditating buddha

Nine foreign coins: including five British West African
coins, one flattened U.S. penny, one French coin

Single feather

Light pink stones

A gray and red stone, sponge-like

Green and pink painted plastic fingertip

Cluster of worry beads and stringed bead necklaces: Stone
bead necklaces: one mostly yellow cylinders; one black,
yellow, and red necklace with mother of pearl Indian head
pendant; two necklaces of purple flat cylinders; one
turquoise bead; one of green, white, and red cylinders;
two of small beads, many green; one green striped orbs;
one of red oblong stones. Miscellaneous necklaces: one
green with yellow striped beads; one heavy metal
cylinders; one of beads made from U.S. dimes; one of
ornamented silver orbs; brown plastic rosary; one green
plastic beads; one multicolored, faceted, gemlike beads;

one silver chain; one light blue bead rosary; African-style yellow, black, and red beads on leather; one of multicolored stones, plastic, clay; plastic reed heart with yellow squiggles pendant on string. Red tissue paper.

Skull pins with rhinestones for eyes

Stone carving and glass crystal

Green beach glass

Magnifying eyepiece

Circle pin

Eleven images of religious figures, from Tibetan monks in prayer, to a St. Jude prayer card, with writing on back: To David, you are wonderful, Love (illegible) *toy horse in yard*

My daughter had been asking for a farm set for some time. Re-searching toy farms for her fourth birthday present took me deep into the world of animal figurines. I got lost trying to decide whether to collect wooden animal figurines, which are extremely expensive, sometimes as much as twenty dollars apiece, or plastic Schleich figurines, like the dinosaurs she already had. One web-site, called The Modern Mindful Mom, dissects the difference between two of the popular German wooden animal figurines, the Ostheimers and the Holztigers. The Ostheimers are more expensive, and not available on Amazon, but they are considered superior—in part because of their blank expressions, which many believe offer children more room for imagination.

In the end, I decided to follow the toy farm setup described on the Montessori mom blog I devotedly followed at the time: a wooden barn with plastic doors purchased online from Target by my father and aunt, a green felt mat with embroidered plants, paths, and fences I asked them to order from Etsy, and plastic farm animals from Schleich. I even ordered the same two-shelf unit from IKEA, which allows children to play at the farm while standing up, and to store the animals in baskets underneath; I also purchased a similar wooden box with a clasp for the miniature items that can be choking hazards, like the eggs and chicks for the chicken coop.

For my daughter's birthday, besides the barn, the chicken coop, and the mat, I let my aunt decide which initial set of farm animals to select as gifts. This involved another monthslong back-and-forth, as we researched together the various animals. My aunt had many ideas about pairings and groupings—male and female, mother and baby. The complications, she wrote to me then, of toy collectibles. She had a lot of opinions in particular about the horses, which we would later try to create a stable of for Christmas. Later, my father tells me that she collected toy horses as a child—the same type of Breyer horses collected in David Wojnarowicz's archive. My daughter's only request was a white horse. They do sell individual horses, my aunt wrote me, but finding a white one might be difficult, involving searching by breed and gender, not just "horse." But you have to be careful, she warned, as they come in different sizes. Here, for example, she wrote, is the Schleich Horse Club Arabian Stallion, which I think is just slightly smaller than the Schleich Farm World Tennessee Walker Mare, the one we gave her for her birthday. There are Arabs in other colors, too, not surprisingly—a popular breed. There is also a Lippizaner stallion, the only really all-white breed I know, but I don't like the looks of it.

When my daughter recently split her chin open, my aunt and father sent her and her sister two more horse figurines, a full-size and a baby one, which they played with throughout every room, until they relegated them to the basket with the others. At the family cabin that summer, the horses were among the few toys I brought for the girls. When they were not in use I amused myself taking photographs of them staged in various places, including outside, like Joseph Cornell's photo collage of a horse, taken in his own yard—the forlorn absurdity of a toy horse in a natural landscape, like some lilliputian creature.

farm set

My father has taken an active interest in the accumulating farm set. He's intrigued that my daughters play with what he calls "old-fashioned toys," the kind he played with as a child. When he visits for that first Easter, he wants to come inside and watch my daughter play with the farm set, which we allow, although we feel nervous about it, as we haven't let anyone inside since the pandemic, and the children aren't yet able to be vaccinated. Earlier in the winter, he had decided that he wanted to buy more toy animals. I eagerly made a list, thinking of the zoos she is already building, making enclosures with wooden blocks, or to fill in the needed language objects, or to teach ecosystems, or geography, or for her to draw. For a while I tried to find toy versions of animals they'd seen at the zoo, in Prospect Park or in the Bronx—the small red panda, the rhino, the giraffe, which the toddler always holds next to the page in *Corduroy* showing the toy giraffe on the shelf next to the teddy bear. I could get them the forest animals they might see at the cabin, like a bear or a deer or even a turkey if they were available.

But my father is determined to get only farm animals, even though we already have plenty, and he wants to pick them out himself, most likely peering over my aunt's shoulder at her computer on Sundays when he's over for dinner. Most of the Schleich animals we want are out of stock on Amazon, or they're price-gouged, or they've already become aftermarket collectibles, as my aunt puts it. I have a photograph of my father holding my daughter, his youngest grandchild, a baby in a sweet brown romper, at the children's farm at the Prospect Park Zoo. The photo was taken in May, a second trip after that first pandemic Easter. He is trying to show her the llama. It was so hot, that May, while it's now so rainy and cool, the May when I am writing this. We had just been on the carousel, with its Victorian wooden horses (and a lion, a giraffe, and a deer)—the girls together with their cousins, and my sister. Schleich, however, does not sell llamas in its farm collection. It does sell toy goats, and goats can be seen at the children's farm, and fed with pellets bought with quarters from a machine. But now my father doesn't like the look of the goat, my aunt tells me, so he refuses to get it. She finally orders from the Schleich site. We settle on another pig, so she can have a set; a donkey; the sheep and lamb; a small male mallard, like the ones on the lake at the cabin; a dog; and another matching cow and calf. Although my father was determined to get only farm animals, my aunt throws in a zebra, which is good for learning the Z in our last name. Just yesterday, on a family walk, I found the plastic duck in my jacket pocket.

The animals are part of a gift economy for my father, an exchange. Earlier that winter, I had spent weeks trying to figure out how to get him vaccinated in Chicago, checking the Walgreens site all day—often at 3 a.m., when I was up nursing. Finally I was able to reason with a young pharmacist named Joanna at a Walgreens near where I grew up. I explained that my father, an eighty-year-old man whose cancer was only recently in remission, was a longtime employee at the corporate offices, now retired. Could he in any way be considered for the employee vaccine day? If he showed up first thing and no one was there, she told me, they could probably do it. All the drama and dread that early February day when he was scheduled to get the shot of Pfizer, when he was snowed in—finally we urged him over the phone to call a cab, which he actually did. Later, he wanted to go back with chocolate and flowers for Joanna, to thank her, until I convinced him not to.

cellar logic

When we last saw my father and my aunt, on their Easter visit, we mentioned that the five-year-old was starting to get interested in weaving and knitting, that we might want to buy her a small lap loom this summer, or make one out of cardboard; we also mentioned that her father is interested in weaving. We spoke about our interest in the fiber artist Lenore Tawney, from Lorain, Ohio, where we have family, although I think they have all died in recent years, my grandmother's baby sister and her family. It turns out there is a very large loom from the 1950s that my grandfather bought my grandmother, which used to occupy the entire spare room on the second floor. The loom is still in the basement, in a box the size of a refrigerator. Did we want it? my father and aunt seemed to ask collectively. We all laughed, wondering how we would ever get that to Brooklyn, and where we would put it if we did.

When I asked my father what else was in the basement, he retold the story, as he usually does, that at one point he had to throw out seven old televisions that were stored down there. Sofia and I have been exchanging emails on hoarding versus collecting. Hoarding, I muse, is about ugliness. Yes! she writes me back.

Ugliness as well as shame. Collecting, perhaps, is about beauty, I suggest. An organizing spirit. At some point, Joseph Cornell's organizing of his cellar at his family house in Queens, which he made into his workshop, became as much a part of his art as the construction of his collages and boxes. In a diary entry from March 1959, he wrote of this cellar logic:

Creative filing
Creative arrangement
As poetics
As technique
As joyous creation

I am struck by the black-and-white archival images of this basement studio space, which show stacks of storage boxes, painted white with dark lettering, containing the raw materials of what would become his art. The boxes are labeled and arranged so that they seem to form a list. I try to read them:

Notions	Dürer
Metal Discs	Cordials
Plastic Shells	Owl Cut-Outs
Old-Fashioned Marbles	Tinted Curio Glasses
Compasses	Springs
Sea-Shells	Map Tacks
Bird Feathers	Dried Pigments
Watch Parts	Glasses
Tinfoil	Balls/Corks
Medici Slot Machines	Wooden Balls Only

I think of the model train set his brother, Robert, whom he took care of, played with in their living room. My father tells me that he and his own twin brother played with an elevated model train set in their basement—a train set that included a built-in farm set. In the same basement were boxes full of my aunt's Breyer model horses and collectibles. I think of Cornell and my father in their houses alone, my aunt in the house where she grew up alone after their brother and mother died. The deep historical sadness of this, these two houses stuffed entirely with objects.

In October, when my father and aunt visit, they bring my grandfather's heavy still camera, which I had asked for. He had a darkroom, off to the side of the kitchen. My aunt makes me promise that if I ever decide I don't want it anymore I will give it back to her. It was buried in the closet, she tells me. Her father had died weeks before her eighth birthday. If there's film inside, it's long since degraded, she warns me. I'm struck by this—my aunt, an old woman, older even than her years, still halted by the sudden death of her father when she was only eight. She never moved out of the house. That need to be at home with childhood objects and her father's things.

Over Christmas, I ask my father about the felt advent calendar my mother made, which had brought me such delight as a child. You'd have to find it in the crawl space, he says, I'm not going in there anymore.

language objects

The youngest one now opens one of the tiny wooden boxes that hold miniatures. She kisses these tiny objects—the tinier the object, the more likely she is to kiss it. Oh baby, sometimes she will say, when she tries to kiss a tiny thimble or a tiny collection of strawberries in a basket.

Originally I collected these miniatures for her older sister, intending to use them during her year at home as language objects, which is a Montessori (or Montessori-adjacent) concept I gleaned online. The idea was to collect small objects, at least one for every letter, hopefully several, in order to teach first-stage phonics, as I tried to teach my daughter to read. I gathered some of the smaller animals as language objects, as well as plastic toys like the tubes of plastic insects and bugs, even little plastic human organs, or the plastic sea creatures we used at bath time. The idea is to put three of these objects on a tray and ask, Which of these begins with la la la? Then, hopefully, she picks the ladybug. Eventually we graduate to trays devoted to one letter, and three objects beginning with that letter. My email is full of threads to myself working out an alphabetic index to make sure I had enough language objects. Some of these I had rounded up and others I was potentially considering. The idea, suggested the blog, was to continually scout for these. It looks something like this:

A	apple, ant, angel
B	bottle, banana, bus
C	car, caterpillar? carrot (wooden), cup, cow
D	dinosaur (that's big), doll, dragonfly, duck
E	eel (sea creatures), egg, elephant
F	fish (wooden), flower
G	grasshopper, goat
H	hippo, hot dog
I	insect, igloo
J	juice bottle, jewel
K	kangaroo, key
L	lizard, ladybug
M	monkey, mushroom
N	nest

O	orange
P	penguin, pig, puzzle
Q	quarter, Q-tip, quartz, question mark?
R	rhino, ribbon, rooster, rainbow
S	shark, seal, starfish (sea creatures), spider
T	turtle, tiger, teacup, tree
U	unicorn, umbrella
V	vegetable, vase (or could get a $13 musical instrument set to get a violin)
W	whale
X	xylophone
Y	yarn?, yoyo
Z	zebra, zipper

Some of these miniatures, which are essentially inexpensive doll-house miniatures packaged for this purpose, I ordered on Etsy for twenty-six dollars. In a note to the seller I asked if I could have the tiny rubber map instead of a marble, as I was worried then about the baby choking, and also the tiny igloo and even a very tiny fried egg (I don't remember what they were replacing). For a while we worked with these language objects every day. Then we stopped, and I just let her take the box out and play with the objects herself, inventing all these imaginative worlds. Now her baby sister is the one who wants to play with the language objects.

And here I am too, in a way, playing with these language objects.

DIY sound object box

The other day, I sat half listening as the two girls paged through a book together. The book was filled with illustrations of animals and objects. The big sister would point to the object and say the word, and the little sister would repeat it, as now she can pronounce most words and even point out the names of animals. It was so strange listening to them, intoning the words as if they were making some sort of Dada poem. Orange. Lightbulb. Bottle. Sink. Sunglasses. Ghost. Fire. Chain saw.

The younger one has started being able to say the "s" and "sh" sounds, although she sometimes confuses them. She sings a song about the sun, but says "shun": Shun, shun, shine down on me. I remember the squabble John and I got into the previous winter, as he observed me trying to work with our daughter on the language objects. When we came to the figure of a shark, I made the "sss" sound, because the word begins with S, but he insisted that that was confusing, that I should say "sh sh sh shark." The "sh" sound is a digraph, apparently, and that's a later stage.

I remember now the post on the Montessori blog about how to DIY a Sound Object Box, an exercise in which the child places small objects in a box corresponding to the initial sound of the object's name. This is one of those homeschooling crafts that sound simple but in fact are maddeningly labyrinthine. All you need to do is find a wooden box with twenty-five compartments at a thrift shop (presumably X would share with another letter)—the mom paid four dollars for hers—and paint the letters on it with acrylic paint, then affix the box to the wall with hanging strips. The child can take the box off the wall to work, then hang it back on the wall when finished. So simple. Ideally of course you have room to create a learning nook, with a bowl of plastic animals and other language objects kept below the box, an idea I became fixated upon for a while. Where would we find room, where would we have a foot of space to create a nook like that? That winter at home I found myself reading this post over and over again, trying to figure out how, when I wasn't going inside stores, I could possibly find a quaint vintage wooden box with twenty-five compartments, of just the right size, and how the system would actually work. It seemed impossible, and at some point I gave up.

As I was recently looking at the original post, I realized that the DIY Sound Object Box closely resembled a Victorian shadow box, a glass-fronted wooden cabinet of the kind Joseph Cornell used to create his boxes, especially his painted dovecotes of tiny objects. In nineteenth-century Europe and America, I read online, the crafting of a shadow box, usually by women, was a way to collect dried flowers and other mementos, "sentimental objects, intended to preserve an atmosphere or a particular time or person." This was also a box practice, like Wojnarowicz's Magic Box or Cornell's shadow boxes, private as well as in some ways for display. These artists made collecting and organizing their own art form, grappling with objects from the past by organizing them into new constellations. In an online exhibition for a Cornell museum show, I find a photo of an epic Victorian shadow box, a large wooden cabinet with tiny boxes containing tiny objects. There are myriad collections of miniature perfume bottles and decanters, filled with colored liquid. So many tiny ceramic, glass, and crystal birds, including owls and swans. The smallest bubble-gum machine. A miniature Santa Claus, like the one in Wojnarowicz's Magic Box. The objects are so tiny, I wonder how any adult fingers could have placed them inside their small compartments. I think of my daughters, how they would delight in them.

I too ache to catalogue these objects, to preserve them in language. Why? Perhaps because they are so tiny. I try and then I give up.

TRANSLUCENCIES

a calendar or notebook

(AFTER BERNADETTE AND ROSEMARY MAYER)

Documentation of Balloon for a Birthday

A photograph of children at a birthday party is always in the present tense. This one, a photograph of two sisters in front of Lefferts Historic House in Prospect Park, was taken in 1957. They might be in the middle of a birthday party. Maybe they are just having a special day out. Other children and adults are just outside the frame, partially visible and in shadow. They are little girls, possibly two and six years of age, as her own daughters were now; they are elderly now, if they are alive at all. They are wearing frock coats, for a special occasion, and hats with earflaps. The trees are bare, but there is no snow on the ground, so it is most likely late fall or early spring. Their expressions are inscrutable, possibly impatient, the kind of look children give adults trying to keep them still to take their photograph. The oldest carries a balloon, and she is eating something from a box, perhaps popcorn or candy. The photograph is black-and-white, but the balloon must be red.

Balloon, her younger child now says, pointing to the red balloon in *Goodnight Moon*, a bedtime story old enough that these other girls might also have read from it, if they spoke or read English.

The Gottlieb girls. Their parents were survivors of Auschwitz and Dachau as children. They met in a displaced persons camp in Naples, where the eldest, Madeline, was born. Roland Barthes: Is there anything sadder than a historical photograph of a child? The sisters are in the park's newly built Children's Corner, next to the zoo. They would have been staring at the carousel recently brought over from Coney Island, built by Charles Carmel in the flamboyant Coney Island style. The horses, with real horsehair tails, in gold, silver, and jewels, the dragon chariots, a lion, a giraffe, a deer with real antlers. Perhaps the Gottlieb girls got to ride it.

Next to the carousel, in a later century, not a photograph but a video. Two children jump in a mud puddle. They are wearing cloth masks. They are just four years old. The girl, whose birthday it is, jumps over and over in the mud, not caring if she splatters her friend. When he runs away, looking to be consoled by his mother, the girl looks momentarily concerned, then proceeds, stomping merrily. She is not wearing the proper shoes or rain gear; she will have to be carried out of the park with bare feet. The video will be shared over and over again, disseminated to family who have not seen her in some time, as well as to friends. A moment of pure being. Later that day, a photograph of the girl with her hands on her face, staring in wonder at the glow of candles on a homemade cake, white with rainbow sprinkles, inedible but still pretty.

Then, a full year later, another birthday, this time a much-promised party. Children run around in their parkas, now accustomed to freezing birthday parties in the open air. Later they gather around on the concrete back steps, trying to hand the child whose birthday it is their presents to open. The birthday child is wearing a crown. A few adults stand nearby, helping and watching. Such nostalgia to this photograph. The energy of their bodies. The different fits and colors of their puffer coats, as it's already cold. Some of the coats are snug, as the parents try to squeeze one last season out of them, others are a size up, coats that will hopefully last at least another year.

If there is a punctum to this photograph, a detail that is a prick or wound, it might be the fact that this photograph could have been taken in so many eras. Unless the punctum is the occasional mask, still worn outside, insisted on by uncommonly vigilant parents. All the parents seem worn out, the mothers especially. It is the mothers who plan the parties. It was nothing, they say when complimented—an affected ease, when the planning and organization was near constant. Don't buy cupcakes, just make them, it's so easy, these same mothers will say. Even when keeping it comparatively simple (read: inexpensive), there absolutely must be juice boxes, candy, granola bars, "snacks," if the party takes place off hours; if during lunchtime, the more expensive, expected boxes of pizza—or, in this case by a mother who is as usual trying too hard, dumplings, separated onto different platters to distinguish between vegetarian and meat, as denoted by either a wooden mushroom and onion for veggie, a cow and a pig figurine for beef and pork. The theme to this late fall birthday party is "animal," vaguely, so there are paper animal masks for the kids to wear while running around, a game of pin-the-tail-on-the-elephant drawn on butcher paper taped to the fence.

Each party bag contains a miniature plastic animal, with baby animals for the toddler siblings, along with a craft project and candy. The bags were put together in an assembly line the night before: twenty wooden stars from an online craft store ordered months earlier, glitter glue, pom-poms, a little paintbrush and a container of paint, a lollipop and candy, all in a muslin bag stamped with the child's name in blue, all ideas lifted entirely from a blog run by an art teacher, except the plastic animals, which proved more costly, and as always, a little overdone. The bags, the mother tries to tell people, can be used for collecting leaves. There are fall leaves gathered in a basket on a small table, along with chalk markers for decorating, a variation on the usual painted miniature pumpkins. There is also a table for painting a birthday banner. Mostly the children mill around and talk, open their bags and start eating the candy. HAPPY BIRTHDAY, the felt banner announces, draped from the fence above the snack table, saved from the prior year. The adults talk about their children and the timing of their vaccines.

Later the mother's friend, whom she used to see every week in the park during the year at home, the one whose son was trying to avoid getting splashed with mud, will send her own photos from the party. So many photographs, which will be sent on to grandparents and family who are not there. Is that partially what the party was for? To show her child how loved she was? To show others who are not there? Or to try to soothe some child-hood trauma—her child's or her own?—as with all her decisions these past two years? The photographs are beautiful in their slight variations. "An image of light and shadow streaming

over faces," Annie Ernaux writes of childhood photographs in
The Years.

The mother will be so glad to see this friend, whom she hasn't
seen since school began, since each left town briefly in August to
visit family. Seeing this friend again, she will feel overcome with
emotion. Why is it, she wonders the next day, suddenly depressed and exhausted, weeping to the point of translucence, that
the only time she sees other mothers with children the same
age—or anyone, for that matter—is outside, on dreary, rainy
days, in a backyard or in the park, for birthday parties? She
thinks of last year: the showing up, the same small community of
parents with children at home. There was an alienation now as
children scattered to other schools. Her friend, for example, was
annoyed when the weekly playdate with her son ended because
the other mother had enrolled her daughter in a cooperative preschool in the park later that spring, and then in summer camp, so
that the mother might somehow write a book, and even more
annoyed to hear that she was spending the entire proceeds of a
fellowship on two years of her daughter's new school, not putting her daughter in a public kindergarten, as the friend was doing with her son, albeit at one that required her to travel daily
into Manhattan, a choice that would put the children in different
grades in school, though they were born only two weeks apart.
What was the point, she imagined this mother thinking, of continuing to know each other, then? Always the question: Who
to keep in touch with? What friendships could be continued?
What is community? They would text each other how much they
missed each other, and make plans to see each other again, to

have another playdate, but during the entire year it will never happen—a rhythm in this current reality, when birthday parties or playdates are planned months in advance and suddenly canceled when someone develops a fever or a cough, when by necessity everything happens outside, or at least for them with a still-unvaccinated toddler. When they all worked too much, commuted too much, to see each other.

She remembered, after seeing her friend, how grounded that first year had felt, although isolating as well. Regular dates in the park, where they could vent to each other, talk about what they were planning for dinner. Worse now that the world had gone on, but they were still in the bubble, only now more alone. The privacy she now felt, and the strain. At least her partner saw other parents during drop-off and pickup, which she usually avoided, avoided the small talk and the fashion show, trying to jealously steal time to prep for classes during the baby's nap. When she does show up she feels like an interloper, an outsider.

When she and her partner were allies, they would often gossip lightly about the parents at this new school. Everyone else appears to have more help, they say to each other, but they hide it. So-and-so has a secret nanny, has been doing indoor playdates this entire time, has parents that help, can afford the full astronomical tuition because of inherited wealth. They preferred the queer and gender-nonconforming parents, and felt closer to, or at least aspired to be more like, these parents, compared to the straight couples who seemed almost as a rule to follow depressingly oppressive divisions of labor, and gendered constraints for their own children—disappointing, though maybe not surprising, for such a progressive school.

For this party, besides her friend's son, she has tried to invite only children in the neighborhood. A couple of the children also went to her daughter's school, also taking a train and a shuttle to get there. These were mostly other families who rented apartments, as opposed to the children who lived closer to the school, who often lived in their own brownstones and had second places upstate. Perhaps that was what this party was for, she wondered later, to somehow reconnect with the neighborhood, to offer up their backyard to them—a space that was so rarely in use, mostly because of the landlord's never-finished construction projects, as well as an ongoing problem with the rats.

She had only the fuzziest memories of her own birthdays as a small child. She rarely had birthday parties, mostly because her birthday was the day before New Year's Eve. She vaguely remembers one party, in their living room, the girls in dresses and stockings and patent leather shoes, dancing the bunny hop to a record. And a photograph she remembers seeing, of children at a table at a restaurant, eating ice cream sundaes. Maybe one of these was her fifth birthday. She asked her father, who didn't remember. She wonders whether there was less planning then, less trying so hard to make their children happy. Or was this another example of maternal labor and care erased and forgotten over time?

Often at these parties a balloon is given away, from a floating bouquet tied to a table. More than any other toy, a balloon would occupy the children; once it lost some of its helium they would play game after game of never-let-it-touch-the-ground, until it popped or deflated. The next week, her child's actual birthday, she got a metallic foil balloon shaped like the number 5, from the dollar store, and a handful of smaller balloons. A photograph, taken from the couch, of her daughter coming in through the front door, clutching her 5 balloon, almost levitating with joy, her younger sister toddling after, mouth agape in wonder. The smaller balloons soon fell to the floor, but the 5 remained on the ceiling for a week.

All the birthday balloons that fall reminded the mother of the artist Rosemary Mayer's "temporary monuments," her durational sculptures from 1977, metallic streamers floating from a rooftop or an open field. Sometimes her own breasts reminded her of balloons—how they inflate and soften when drained, how they often serve as pillows for her ever-growing child who is still so often on top of her, even as she prepares for constant lectures and classes. She writes this to her friend Sofia. I wonder about all of the dread and anxiety you write me you're feeling, Sofia responds, and the idea of balloons—is there some connection there? Or a working through slantwise? The pressure, the lack of space/air, the dense feeling—can it then somehow become a buoyancy?

For the party, to add some light, she takes an iridescent origami star—a star she got free in a catalogue—and hangs it out back, from the bare Japanese maple, letting it twirl in the wind. Then, in the weeks ahead, she moves it to the ceiling of the front porch, like mistletoe. Through the winter months she watches it catch the light from the window, often taking videos of it twirling in the wind, until finally the snow squall in February decimates it.

Bustletown

These past two years she has been thinking of the illustrated German picture books called *All Around Bustletown*, where the denizens of an apartment block go about their days, their lives shaped by the seasons. She now reads it to her youngest, waiting for her on the play toilet. The characters shop and take trains, go to birthday parties at the park. Right before Halloween, for the costumed birthday party at the park with new classmates, the mother practiced making batlike squiggles on her daughter's face, her hair in earlike coils on her head, the father glue-gunning cardboard ears onto a headband with black construction paper and wire. The mother is glad her daughter still asks to be a bat, or a pirate, and not a princess or a mermaid, like the older girls in her class, who spend much of the day, her daughter tells her, wrapping themselves up in silk scarves and lying around as mermaids. Sometimes they invite her, and sometimes they don't, oscillating whims and attentions that make her ecstatic or weepy when she comes home, exhausted from navigating this new social stratum.

The father took the girls to the actual birthday party, as the mother had to moderate a panel on literary translation over Zoom, her computer perched on her daughter's tiny transparent desk, removing her various collections and gatherings from the shelves beforehand. Afterward, feeling compelled to show up to say hello to the parents, she arrived to find her older daughter collapsed on the ground in pain. Rolling her pants legs up revealed two hot and swollen knees—a symptom, she would learn later at urgent care, of "serum sickness," from the amoxicillin prescribed to treat the strep throat that had kept her out of school for a week, treated with steroids, which in turn had made her manic; within an hour she went from being almost unable to walk to running laps throughout the apartment, then unable to sleep. Lifting the weeping bat up, the mother carried her out of the park.

During the translation panel, Jenny McPhee, the translator of Natalia Ginzburg's *Family Lexicon*, which had been so important to the mother the previous winter, said something about how everyone speaks about the father's booming voice in Ginzburg's book, but to her the mother's voice is equally important.

The constant dreadful strep all that second year. Viruses but not the virus, at least not yet. Newly fragile immune systems, not used to so many people. The baby is too congested to nurse; they torture her, attempting to clean out her nose with the sucking device. Strings of snot pulled from her nose. Almost pleasurable, the elasticity. Like time, it stretches. The mother could write, after this year, a thesis on snot, on its textures and viscosity. A sense of exile, no one to ask for help, no one else who cares when the children are sick. Natalia Ginzburg wrote, "We love our children in such a painful, frightening way that it seems to us we have never had any other neighbor. . . . Where's God now? We only remember to talk to God when the baby's ill."

During this period when they are stuck at home, the children miserable with bursts of maniacal energy, everyone's sleep disturbed, the mother wakes up and sorts through the closets, everything on the floor, trying to find winter clothes that still fit; hopefully the woolen long underwear will last one more year. She puts together crates of outgrown baby clothes to give away, to their beloved teacher from the forest school, who is expecting her first. The melancholy of this, of foreclosing a third child. But of course—it was an impossibility. There is no space. Not enough money, even now. Finally a check has cleared, and they run around paying for things: a check to send to school, gloves and winter hat for the older one, last year's cannot be located. Always when a check clears—a freelancing or translation check from the heavens—she can buy the children clothes, can replace constantly shrinking leggings and sweatpants and T-shirts.

After years in various earth tones chosen by her mother, the kindergartener now has feelings, constantly in flux, about what colors she will wear. Sometimes she will only wear blue, even if it's a too-small blue T-shirt and blue leggings. For a spell, no clothes that were red. She will only wear, she tells her mother, blue, purple, or pink. Then, for a little bit, she relents and accepts red, if it's monochromatic—red sweatshirt, red socks, red overalls.

The mother wakes up on school mornings and she's head of communication. Before drinking her morning water, like a lady in waiting, waiting to see if she will be needed to help pick out clothes, not knowing when her daughter might insist on autonomy, or insist on her socks being tugged on, brushing hair, observing the brushing of teeth. The father is in the kitchen packing lunch, making breakfast. Sometimes, after being home after an illness, the child will weep and say she doesn't want to go. A childish voice in the kitchen. "At school, everyone always tells me what to do."

Her child always keeps track of the next festival or holiday, wanting to know their order, which one is next, how soon, needing joyful disruptions of the routine. For Halloween night itself they make their own animal masks, this time out of cardboard, that they glue onto dowels to hold up before their faces. The mother and daughter are both nocturnal, the daughter observes— a bat and an owl. Then a lion and an elephant. They invite neighborhood kids to sit on the porch and pass out candy, through a chute made of PVC tube and strung with fairy lights. For the holiday, the children are freed from the alienating daily protocols, wearing, almost subversively, masks on their faces and not over their mouths. This year the haunted houses in the neighborhood are back, including the plague-doctor spectacle two doors down. The welcomed pageantry, a way for the children to find wonder and also to face fear. She imagines historical photos of children trick-or-treating in their neighborhood would still look something like this.

They go from house to house with their friends, the children of the same age whose mother runs the forest school they went to all the previous year. This other mother, who studied art, planned elaborate fairy costumes for her two daughters, with battery-powered lights strung in tulle skirts and painted crowns. Her parents attended as well, wearing matching crowns like the other parents, assisting with the stroller—a miracle, to have grandparents who lived nearby. The two mothers will smile at each other as they wear their now-exhausted toddlers across the busy night street, teeming with children, their breasts peeking out to nurse. The two older girls hold hands and chat animatedly about candy. For days afterward, the only topic of conversation will be the contents of that candy bag. She and the other mothers text one another images of their children in their costumes—the pride at putting one together, the relief she feels, as she is often a pure failure at anything resembling craft. A friend texts her a close-up of ruby-red shoes. I have glitter all over me, she writes.

The blurriness of a photograph, taken outside on Halloween, illuminated by the lights in the other child's blue tulle skirt. The other mother, also the documentarian of her family, will send countless, nearly identical photographs the next morning. As the mother scrolls through the photos of her children, she thinks of Diane Arbus taking the bus to New Jersey, to a home for the developmentally disabled, photographing the residents wearing plastic masks, carrying homemade fairy wands with stars pasted on top. For years the mother has tried to capture the spooky and melancholy, almost ecstatic, light of these black-and-white photographs in language, never knowing quite how to describe them. She has been drawn lately to thinking of artists with two daughters—Diane Arbus, Bernadette Mayer. That line in Arbus's appointment book: "Buy Amy's birthday present, go to morgue."

Charmed by the girls running around the next days with the cardboard animal masks. Something magic to it, to the constant make-believe and dress-up. The baby making roaring sounds, the same sound for any animal. It will never be like this again, she realizes—so sweet and so awful.

During the fall in Bustletown there is a lantern festival for the kindergarteners, with handmade lamps, much like the lantern festival near the grandmother tree at Fort Greene Park for her daughter's school in late autumn, a way to greet the new winter darkness with light. That week children brought in mason jars, large enough for the teacher's hand to reach inside and place a tealight, each jar decorated with gold sparkle stars and painted tissue paper. They learned songs the children would sing for weeks, as if they too were in a German picture book. Glimmer, lantern, glimmer, her daughter sings. The photos of the children in their puffers, holding their lanterns. The coloration of that particular winter uniform of her daughter's that will never re-peat. How much care the mother took picking it out, and how she spent inevitably too much. The expenses of winter clothing— the new and special burgundy pom-pom hat, the burgundy puffer. The hearts on the knitted woolen gloves. The pink wool overalls with holes and dirty knees. All these rituals, the whole kooky tradition, which she was taking on even more work to afford, to provide for her daughter this absurd and probably futile ideal, as if she could meet some impossible longing with the glow of these lights, the magic of it.

How crazy is it? another mother asks of her daughter's school, as they stand in the backyard of her brownstone later that spring, where she is hosting her daughter's sixth birthday party, in a rapidly gentrifying neighborhood in central Brooklyn. The season of the outside birthday party has returned. Her manageable gift this season has been a box of beeswax crayons, wrapped up in a painting or drawing her girls made that morning, together at the table. Four or five children were racing around, masks now off outside, then back on as soon as they went through the sliding glass doors and back inside to have cake, then masks off to eat—an elaborate cake in the shape of a train, which of course the mother said was nothing, no work at all. Their daughters used to attend the forest school at the Nethermead together. They haven't seen each other since her own daughter's late November birthday. The birthday girl goes to an in-demand charter school, where the enrollment works by lottery, or in her case because siblings attended the school, which they love, she says. It's basically a forest school, she goes on, they spend all their time outside. Some homework but not too much. And it's very diverse. Everyone here talks about how good their situation is, but in their telling, she's noticed, it's always undercut with defensiveness, perhaps uncertainty. She always liked this other woman—liked how no-nonsense she usually was, how good she was with children. Which part do you mean? the mother now asks. Not the nuttiness of theosophy, it turns out, or Rudolf Steiner's poisonous theories about race—rather, the woman is interested in whether the school feels cultlike (a little, she replies), and whether they wait to teach them to read and write. More important, she wants to know about the school's legendary prohibition on screen time. She tells the woman that the teacher did make them promise to do a March media detox, which they were just finishing, because of how often the children spoke about television and movies. She doesn't add that her daughter actually did seem more capable of imaginative play afterward, that she had stopped talking mostly about TV characters, had stopped asking to watch something. That month she lost that one hour of silence, during the baby's nap, in which she could actually think. Just give them a box! the teacher had admonished them during their Zoom call. Although the mother was fairly well-versed in setting up open play, having homeschooled their daughter during her prior year at home, the parents still found this funny. When the girl started zigzagging all over their apartment, or complaining that she was bored, they would sometimes gesture gleefully at the overflowing recycling bin and cry, Just give her a box! And often they actually did just that, gave her a small box and told her that her teacher had said she should play with it. Don't worry, we have so much work to do and no childcare, but just give her a box!

The truth she should have told this other mother was that it was all crazy—of course it was crazy, it was all so fucking crazy. But that's not what she was asking.

Midwinter Day

It was during that fall that she tried, finally, to work on the girls' room. She had a desire to make the room cheerful and bright. She composed impassioned communications to their landlord, asking if they could paint the walls, which were yellowing and peeling, full of holes from construction upstairs, where a radiator pipe had pulled through the wall and was hastily plastered over and left lumpy and unpainted. She looked up paint colors. Soft shell seemed soothing, like a peach. Perhaps she was thinking of the soft peachy-pink walls, painted in the translucent lazure wash, in her daughter's new classroom. The parents were allowed inside only once, on the first day of school, because of the new protocols. The room felt so soothing, so beautiful. Everything arranged in such a calm way, in baskets, all the felt and large blocks for building house and store.

Finally the landlord agreed to paint the walls, but only plain white. She ordered wall decals for the room, a rainbow for above the bed and a sun above the crib. We've been rainbow-pilled, she joked to her partner. Her own father, the children's grandfather, had offered to buy a proper bed for the older child, whose feet were nearly sticking out of her current bed. He couldn't believe they were still living as they were, the older daughter still in a convertible toddler bed that was once her crib, the toddler still in a mini crib in their room, where she would remain for another year. It was a complex geometry problem, figuring out how to

add a twin-size bed into the room—which used to be her office—
along with the toddler bed, now converted back into a crib. Have
you figured out the bed yet? her father needled whenever they
spoke. Finally, the dresser was moved in front of the radiator,
and the two beds barely fit. The large bedroom had long been
the domain of her older daughter, who jealously guarded it against
intruders. Her little sister couldn't go there to play, even during
the day. At night, her daughter began a prolonged ritual of putting every doll and object on the floor to bed—brushes got beds,
books got beds—and she would be enraged if this mystifying
system was disturbed. Suddenly, now all of their living during
the day was in the living room, their dim, often dingy shared
space.

So she became fixated on lighting. Making sure all the lights were
on when they woke up, opening the blinds on the small windows
in the girls' room in the morning. This became her obsession,
that fall and winter, trying to find light in the apartment they had
lived in for a decade. Moving what lamps they had into other
rooms, seeing if that helped. Installing cheap light sconces in the
bedroom, fixtures that looked large and out of place, but at least
she could now read in bed. She wondered what stage of the pandemic she had reached when she found herself longing for pink
linen curtains. A desire to wake up in the morning, washed in
pink, in one's pastel bed. They had no money for such improve-
ments, having allocated the entirety of her fellowship checks to
her daughter's school, and summer camp, and partially for their
health insurance. Yet still she was able to place, sometime that
winter, a much-debated IKEA order of twenty-dollar translucent

curtains for the three windows in the front room, gray blinds to replace broken ones in the girls' room (one of which promptly broke, replaced with a silk scarf on a dowel), and three paper lanterns, which remain under their bed, uninstalled, six months later.

That late fall and winter, a renewed obsession with the diminishing light, both inside and out, the cast of a gray painting. Trying to still find charm and delight in the atmosphere. The fairy lights on the tree moved over to the window grate. The iridescent star still hanging outside. The video of the baby painting with a fluorescent yellow tempera cake—the gesture where she decided to make a mark, then to drip the water, swirl, then paint her skin, press her mouth to the yellow, face glowing.

No money in January, after Christmas and birthdays, so pleasure was had in craft projects. Painted watercolor houses strung on a garland on a dim patch of back wall covering a crack, and a water stain from an upstairs plumbing leak. On New Year's Day, the children made painted crowns from paper bags and glitter-glued on pom-poms. And then a photograph of the girls smiling, wearing their crowns. The crowns went up on the January nature table in front of the window, formerly covered by filthy yellow sheer curtains. Now a taped-on winter blue silk scarf hides the construction debris in the alley, where the rats run past at night, on their way to the neighboring apartment building's overflowing trash. On the table the crystal from the history museum, two of the metallic peg people from the winter fair. Paper snowflakes on collected branches. Tiny red beeswax winterberries made by the kindergartener. A taped-on rainbow Waldorf star made with her father, from kite paper the mother had ordered. Now people know what cult we're a part of, he joked.

"Glimmers," her friend Bhanu wrote to her. The sweet ritual of her daughter holding her hand as they take their blue-hour walks, while the baby, the father, and the dog follow behind. Before Christmas they watch a wreath being hung by a professional on the top floor of one of the large neighborhood houses. The daughter tells her mother, continuing a conversation from the previous winter that the mother was surprised the daughter remembered, that fairies actually do live in their backyard. She knows this because she has found a plastic gemstone, which must have fallen out of a child's pocket during her party. Could we clean it off and place it on the nature table? The nature table excites her daughter, it gives them all something to do. They are already planning for another Valentine's, replacing the winter blue silk scarf with a red-and-light-purple scarf. The baby finds a sparkly blue bead and places it there as well. After Christmas, they add pinecones cut from the door wreath. Two tiny red wooden birds from a game. On Midwinter Day, they pay to go to a light show at the botanic gardens—the Cherry Esplanade transformed, thanks to a techno Muzak soundtrack, into a pulsating field of light.

Still, despite these glimmers, this was the most depressed she had felt since the previous winter, possibly because of the darkness. How private it all felt, the work of parenting, the worry, the exhaustion, the constant labor of nagging, of calming, of mediating between the little ones. So exhausted and burned out, yet still expected to continue. The baby teething, her sister running around late at night. Go to bed! Just go to bed! A desire, sometime after Christmas, to go to the park—their space of sanity all last year—to the sandy section her daughter called the desert. She just wanted to walk in the cold and stare at the sky and feel in the world, as she had the previous winter. But that never happened. Instead, after a fight with her husband and her daughter's meltdown, she escaped outside. Walked in the dark down boulevards to the park. The strangeness of this silence. She considered the warm glow of lights inside the large houses, the tall trees. The flâneuse, she thought, as a burned-out mother, the weeping walking woman, fleeing the scene of her own domesticity.

The desire and impossibility, she thought, again and again, of these past two years. How to describe both the claustrophobia and the abundance of the day. To somehow understand her own interior. On Midwinter Day she read Bernadette Mayer's epic project of dailiness and duration, her digressions, record-keeping, and stream of consciousness, all written on December 22, 1978. While reading it, on the couch all day, often nursing the baby, the mother took her own notes. Baby naked in the kitchen. Delighted with her body. Her vulva chapped. The other daughter with knotty hair. Neither has had her hair washed in more than a week. They are making blueberry muffins with their father. The kitchen is trashed. She floats in and out. Holds the baby on her knee. Wearing wools and long johns, stripped to nothing as the radiator knocks and hisses. Talks to her father, tells him school is canceled because of variant. One month no school now. Her brother is unvaccinated, but her father is unconcerned. Wants to talk to his son-in-law about a new American luxury sedan he's thinking of buying.

"In the dream my daughters Sophie and Marie are always with me," Mayer writes. She writes of dreaming of ordering pom-poms for the girls. The mother is ordering pom-poms, rearranging the play area in the living room. They are inside again. Who to tell or see? Clearing for Christmas toys. Wooden blocks in baskets. They eat the lentil soup they made for the teachers. Move the farm and dollhouse. The baby walking around naked with a plastic bag—hands the mother a wooden banana and a small notebook. She watches her daughter's gorgeous little butt as she waddles away. Dinosaurs lined up on the radiator. The five-year-old wants to play a game where they must guess the animal she is thinking of, a game they play at school, her father always up for it, though the mother gets bored with it. "Marie asks me what do turtles eat, then squirrels, rabbits." They are allowed to ask questions: Is it at the zoo, is it extinct, does it eat meat, does it swim? And so on. Watching them play together, in costumes, tutus, superhero masks from birthday parties, polar bear ears. They dance to music, to anything. Running, running. Secrets—let's not tell our parents. This was the mother's longing, that even in this isolation having a sister would feel to her daughter like abundance, not deprivation. They are already a pair. Tramping back and forth on the floor, giggling, pulling the wooden animal toys, being pushed around in a repurposed cardboard box. The house is such a mess, constant laundry, constant running after the toddler. Scurrying around picking up from the floor a million little pieces—socks, doll shoes, sticks, beads, doll bottles, peg people, play dough, toy animals, long underwear, books, wooden balls, board books. They make a mess—she cleans it up. Dust bunnies, stickers, wooden play food, pom-poms, cards from their rolled fruit-leather strips, miniature farm animals. They shake out the rugs once a week; the children mill about with tiny brooms. Her life spent picking up things off the floor. She's so tired of cleaning up. Of picking up objects, putting them back. Why she desires systems, all those shelves, baskets, so they learn to put away their own messes. Baskets tucked under each piece of furniture, the couch, every dresser, to store blocks, cars, diapers, slippers, sweaters. The basket of silk scarves they use for costumes, capes, playing mermaids. Baskets of costumes and musical instruments under the dresser. All the work of the past year, attempting to allow open play. Also small parts, code for repurposed trash: the clear plastic bear-shaped animal cracker jar filled with craft sticks, yogurt container with hole cut out to push in puff balls, all scattered yesterday. The recycling overflowing, the guilt at too many packages, too many boxes, they consume too much. The pleasure when it's all picked up, of clearing a mat-size amount of parquet floor to build with blocks. Yet still a little ashamed at how beautiful everything is. The basket of rainbow glass blocks on the radiator in the morning as they build at the window, so the morning light will shine through and project on the floor. The Midwinter Day journal entry ends suddenly, most likely written during a nap, on the couch, with a toddler asleep on top of her.

Vital Matter

That fall, she was supposed to take photographs of her home for a journal that was publishing a piece of her writing, that dealt in some way with her domestic space. The editor wanted photographs to accompany the piece. The mother worried about this all season. A home is so incredibly private, especially a life spent inside with small children. Especially now. Although she took photographs all the time, of her children at home, she felt uneasy about sharing them, except rarely with friends. Sometimes she was fond of her home, and at other times had surrendered to how shabby and cluttered it was. What was it that the journal wanted anyhow? Some idealized interior, a tidied and ordered, almost uninhabited, fantasy? Or did they want photographs of her messy apartment?

She stares at a small blue Post-it on their front door, amused: Her daughter had asked how to spell the word "insane," apparently so she could write down the sentence "My Parents are Insane," after listening to them bicker, most likely about money. But she has forgotten how to write most of the letters. Could any of this be recorded in a photograph? Could the mother photograph the tiny animals scattered all over the apartment, like this duck sitting on a coffee stain, in front of a stack of vintage Semiotext(e) / Native Agents paperbacks on the bookshelf behind the couch? Nothing seemed right.

She now stares at computer cords, at the foot of the couch, wrapped around a desk copy of Jane Bennett's *Vibrant Matter*, which she finally now opens. In it, Bennett writes about the force of things, their political ecology, the "contingent tableau" that forms a spark. All the spare detritus that gathers in corners in the main room: the felt bandage from the play medical kit, a black shoelace, a white washcloth, a play dough lid, a dust bunny. A miniature small intestine from a set of plastic organs, a small maraca from forest school, a crumpled play-money paper dollar—all of this a tableau of junk on the table at 5 a.m. That's what the mother wanted to photograph, the vibrancy of these objects, their collected animal. The dollar might get chewed on and carried through to another room, it might get crumpled up and stepped on and live under a bureau; it might—someday—get thrown out or recycled; it might be put in a dusty little rope bowl with the others, for the constant game of shop, in fact her daughter has a toy cash register for just this purpose, though it remains tucked in the closet in favor of a yoga block she uses as a register and shop desk. Perhaps she will try to sell one of the other magic items. She assigns them all arbitrary values, regardless of size or function: five dollars, please, or eleven dollars, please. The toys that clutter this place, even the trash, already have a history; they are objects of duration. Does the mother want to photograph the ugly things, the ugly vital things? Why transcribe her small domestic space? The desire to record its ongoing coziness without stilling it into a photographable domesticity. That's what she appreciated about the Bustletown books. Each room of the large apartment building was inhabited in a way that showed life was being lived, even outside; there was wet laundry hanging up in the bathroom, dishes piled up in the sink, toys on the floor.

Still, she sends photos to her father and sister, to friends. On Christmas Day the little girl happily on her sister's lap, in their cheerful tomato-red pajamas, sitting in front of the small tree at the window, the presents in brown paper packages. Both of them smiling in their little corner. The photograph reminds her of the framed one of her and her sister, now mothers and aunts, in front of the towering Christmas tree, in white tights and dresses from when they were children, about one and two years old. Her own two girls running around now, with blue and red silk scarves tied around them, holding the foam swords she bought them, playing knights. The older sister sitting at her desk, topless, finger-knitting thoughtfully with chunky rainbow yarn. But what the photographs elide. There's no sound, and no movement. Her daughters run around chasing each other, gleefully screaming, angrily screaming, maniacally screaming, back and forth, back and forth. Tears and fights that day, as every day. Crashes. There was almost no break from it, unless they were sleeping. Her older daughter yells that the mother has ruined her Christmas, for some small offense soon forgotten. Of course, she remembers sulking the exact same way to her own mother on Christmas Day. The mother knows she must absent herself, put her feelings on hold, on holidays like this—not to feel grief, not to be selfish, but because this is an intense day, so it risks disappointing. Her sister FaceTimes with her girls from brunch at a crowded London hotel, everyone unmasked. Which makes her daughter pout.

Why don't they ever see family? All they see is each other. The sisters talk about their father, the children's grandfather, who has recently fallen on the concrete outside a crowded restaurant near their childhood home. They won't see one another again until the following Easter, when they can manage to get together, when it's bearable to sit outside.

Building Dwelling Thinking

We don't want to dwell in the pandemic, the magazine editors tell her, referring to writing they will publish that spring. We're hoping by then that we'll be looking outward. But that is what they were still doing, that winter, dwelling in the pandemic. The fortunes they were spending on kids' KN95s and hoarding at-home tests. Keeping their eldest home for much of January, worrying about the positive tests in her small class when the youngest wasn't vaccinated. She handed out tests to the new upstairs neighbors, who test positive, and to a neighborhood friend, whom she hasn't seen all year, who waves when she reaches up to collect the bag she's hung over the fence. The baby puts a hot-pink mask on a baby doll, on herself. This is the new play. Mask, she says, wanting to know why she can't wear one. It's all so unbearably glamorous and interesting, the ugly paper masks they keep on the table near the door—she must climb up to them, go to the mirror and try them on, like lipstick.

Still, there were glimmers. The first snowstorm in January, they rushed to the front window. The girls stood on the radiator and watched it come down. As soon as a check cleared, she ordered snow pants for her daughter and a snowsuit for the baby. She videoed the girls making snow angels out front. Months later, she stood wearing the baby, holding the other's hand, in front of *Memory: Past*, the glittery lavender Howardena Pindell painting at MoMA. Exhausted from carrying the baby all yesterday in Midtown. Pindell's paintings, made partly with paper hole punches, evoking New York City blizzards.

This winter, on walks, they play I Spy, in search of January colors: still red, the winterberries, the leftover red bows, and light. Home again for February break; the more you pay, one parent jokes, the less your child is actually in school. Then the girls are sick again, sick but not sick-sick, just strep and fevers, and so her eldest is home, missing the school Valentine's celebration for which they'd spent the weekend creating handmade valentines, thirteen in all. Her whole being inside her daughters' fevers. Begging for dispensation to teach over Zoom, because her baby is ill. The pink fever flowers on her cheeks. That night, one of her rare escapes onto the porch, the mother watches pink foil heart balloons released into the night sky. Glimmering skyward until they disappear.

When they get better, she takes the five-year-old ice skating. Something to say she did during the February break. Many of her peers are on beaches somewhere. The mother reflects that she never went ice skating as a child. She pulls on a helmet, knee pads, elbow pads, all of it rented—the only adult wearing such gear. She manages to stay thirty minutes on the rink. The next day, every part of her body hurts.

The winter isolates again. It's unbelievable, this February sleep regression. The fatigue is almost gilded. She passes by the bathroom mirror. She sees herself as a smeared woman. Her exhaustion makes her look ancient. The baby will sleep only on her mother's body, or pressed up near it. She wakes up every two hours, to claw at her. At night they lie in the cold bed—the radiator has decided again to not work. In the day her back is sore, as is her hip. In the morning, her partner lets her sleep an hour and she can finally sleep, relaxing her body as she did in childhood, when she had her own bed, her sister in the twin bed across the room. She slept on her stomach, one leg hunched up, the other one stretched diagonally across. She wakes up to the children mewing like cats.

One of her students in her animal lecture tells her that she takes a weekly twelve-hour vow of silence as part of her meditation practice. Does this include sleeping? she asks. Sometimes, she replies. What do you do? she presses, fascinated. She doesn't text or email, the student tells her. Sometimes she writes poetry. She takes walks in Riverside Park and sits on a bench. This would be impossible for me, she says. You should try, she says. But that's not what she means. There is nothing more foreclosed to her than such free time—with children, with students, with deadlines—and yet nothing more desired. Perhaps nap times are that for her, when the other one is in school. Or the occasional hot bath. Children screaming at her door, attempting to come in. Mama, I have to tell you something.

By the time they've been home together for well over one month, with very little school, she is bickering regularly with the five-year-old, who complains that they favor the younger one, give her all the attention. She stomps around, climbs on her parents, collapses in tears. In the morning, she spends all her energy trying to keep her little sister out of the bedroom they're supposed to share. She jumps in her parents' bed, jealous her sister is still there. While there she tells her mother, who is still lying down, her dreams. It was two dreams, she clarifies. In one, she was playing in the playground with her friends, who are in the other class. First they played outside, then inside. They played mice, or was it rats, she didn't remember. What a city-kid game, her father remarks. What's the difference between mice and rats? the mother asks her daughter. Mice are nicer, she says. How did you play? she then asks. Her friend was the baby mouse and they took care of her. Many of their imaginative games seem to hinge on some version of playing family, being caretakers, children, or babies. Baby cats, baby mice. Later that morning she reads the toddler *Goodnight Moon*, with the small house and young mouse she likes to find. She remembers now, when their beloved teacher from the forest school came over to the porch, there to collect baby clothes, how they saw a rat trotting in their alleyway, out even though it was daylight. They all stopped and watched the rat.

Sometimes her phone sends her these mini films, animated together from still photos of her children's faces. The nostalgia of

it overwhelms her, despite how absurd, even invasive, it all is—
these photos floating up on her phone, reminding her constantly
of the previous year. Often now, when a baby face comes up, she
is confused about whose it is, which daughter does it belong to?
Sometimes she goes through the photos on her phone herself,
until she is overtaken by time and memory and the fullness of it
all. That face! That face!

The Linden Tree

In the fall they return to the linden tree, still green. The leaves of
other trees in the Nethermead are already turning yellow and
red. That cyclical feeling, back to the previous autumn. A seven-
week-old baby sleeps in a stroller, his parents paying more attention to his three-year-old brother. And now last year's new
babies are toddling around, even looking up at the tree, hoping to climb it like their big sisters. The communal memory of
this tree, how many children have jumped off it. That feeling,
how resonant: how much is the same since this time last year,
how much has changed. The entire session paid for but rarely
attended—a mistake, as they didn't realize how exhausted their
daughter would be after a day of kindergarten, so there were often breakdowns on the train there or going home, wanting to eat
a snack on the train, her parents saying no, even though few
others were still wearing masks. Wondering whether this is partially the source of her grief, the way children are expected to

follow protocols when adults do not. How horribly unfair it felt. The uneaten lunch in her lunch box at the end of the day suggests the mystery of something unknown: what exactly goes on at school.

Pastel chalks are the new offering today, laid out at the foot of the tree. The older one walks across a pastel log. Her daughter's friend—the only friend remaining from previous iterations of this Tuesday afternoon group, because her mother runs the school—mixes water in a beaker with purple chalk. Unicorn water, they decide. Her child carefully makes a mud pie. They find a worm in the mud. A younger child tries to bury it in wood chips. Her daughter, now the eldest there, tries to fish it out for the child, patiently. Her younger sister wakes up, focuses her bright blue eyes on the rainbow silk unfurling in the wind.

On another day, later on in the season, there are peg people hidden in the knobs and holes of the linden tree, either by the teacher or by other groups of children, it's always a mystery. As the mother and father watch the children play with the peg people, hiding them again in knobs and holes of the tree, for other children, they are reminded of the instruction to make twenty-five fairies for the upcoming winter fair. The mother has already ordered the peg people online—in their "male," more neutral, variation—but they need to be decorated, then placed so that children can find them in the pockets of the pocket fairy, a volunteer adult who walks around with a magical cape full of pockets. A reminder from the head parent of the class: remember, keep the magic alive for the children, the fairies are the ones who make them. Great, more magic that somehow erases maternal time and care, like Santa Claus or the Easter Bunny, she complains to her partner, who laughs, often the only audience for her jokes. So the kindergartener, who still believes passionately in fairies, is called upon to assist the fairies, collecting acorn tops during walks, digging them out from among the cigarette butts and other trash. Twenty-eight peg people painted with metallic watercolors with silver acorn tops and glue-gunned felt wings, delivered at the last minute to the winter fair.

Remembering the return to the Nethermead after the long winter, during that year at home, for the first primavera, or spring. Walking with the beloved teacher, while the children ran off, carrying the rainbow scarf together, giggling. They stopped and considered a fort structure a group of children had made in the midst of a large open field. The teacher said she looked at this and thought, Children were here. The mothers, the same mothers as the fall, watched the children climb on a log together, then together carry a log. The babies crawled off their plastic blankets, put twigs and grass in their mouths. So cold, yet the sun was incredibly bright. The three mothers discussed the chapter book and series they were reading to their daughters: the Wizard of Oz, Little House on the Prairie, Alice in Wonderland, the Moomins. They discussed schools for next year. The other mother on the walk crouched down to show the children a little brown mushroom. Once the hour and a half was over, they started gathering up. As they left the park, the three girls scooted down the hill past the bridge, zooming behind the boathouse to the tunnel. One of the other mothers was best at getting the children to listen, to remember to wait at the various agreed-upon stops: the bench, the weeping willow near the boathouse, where they gather in giggles, then the broad Scottish elm that Marianne Moore helped rescue, then through the tunnel and over to the other side.

On a Tuesday that spring, one of the fathers talks to one of the mothers as they walk down the hill, stop in front of the lake. How little their daughters remember from when they were three, they discuss—even from the previous fall. Was this because of the normal but still strange quality of childhood memory, that an under-five child's brain is changing so fast that memories and selves don't yet cohere? Or is it because of this specific and collective trauma that they can't remember previous seasons— cannot remember, especially, any concept of the before? What does it mean to be a child during this historical crisis, what memories will they have? They have changed; they are taller; the parents all measure how close they now are in size. The change in other people's children is more pronounced, even after a short amount of time—whereas for their own children, whom they see every day, the change is so gradual as to be imperceptible. Look at the three of them, with their candy-colored helmets and scooters, stopping to see the swans at the lake, so green from toxic algae, but somehow still pretty. The baby swans are gone now, and they tell themselves fictions to explain it away. Look at the turtles sunning themselves on the rocks, mostly red-eared sliders whose ancestors were abandoned as pets. Such a picturesque scene. The children do not notice, or understand, the used condom near the turtle, floating in the muck.

The mother remembers volunteering, that Earth Day, to clean up in the park, on behalf of her daughter's cooperative preschool, which took place almost entirely in the park. They were given plastic gloves and a bag and set out hunting trash: cigarette butts, bottle caps, plastic straws, indistinct swirls of paper, candy wrappers, condom wrappers so old the lettering was unrecognizable, even the tiny red plastic flowers gathered around a tree in one of the many playgrounds. Although her preschooler wasn't interested in picking up trash then, the next time they were at forest school, she walked around picking up tiny shards of glass and plastic, handing them to the teacher, who put them in a green plastic doggie bag, which she then slipped into her smock. Watching her daughter collect these fragments reminded her of the calendar pieces of Yuji Agematsu, who walks the streets of neighborhoods throughout the city, where he lives and where he works, and selects bits of detritus: pieces of gum or candy, feathers, wisps of hair, other forms of plastic wrappers, some which may continue to decay together over time after he collects them, like miniature ecosystems, creating work that is both grotesque and beautiful. Agematsu collects the assemblages in the cellophane wrappers of his daily packs of cigarettes, which he calls "zips," then arranges them in calendar-like monthly rows in Plexiglas cases, his way of recording time.

Zip: The girls stop at the water fountain and all take turns, drinking or holding down the button. The mothers chat underneath the blooming redbud, that creepy yet sublime fuchsia flower that grows into the branches. Sometimes, they relent and agree to stop at the playground. Just for a little bit. They look at the three girls, their masks still on, twirling on the tire swing, a tired parent occasionally pushing. If it's okay with everyone, yes, the masks can come off, now that they're no longer in an official setting. When one of the other children's masks comes off, the mother notices, the face revealed is somehow different from what she had imagined.

The family returned to the Nethermead most recently the following May, during a downpour that soaked the field. The redbud had bloomed again. They were there for the maypole celebration for her daughter's school. Difficult to see anyone because of the rain. She made small talk with a parent, who was soaked through in jeans. Earlier she had had trouble finding pants that she could possibly wear, that wouldn't be soaked. They discussed how their children had at least one set of rain clothes, but the adults had almost none. She felt frantic, trying despite the rain to braid the straw into crowns as was the instruction, and to poke through the flowers that were brought for this purpose. Still, she got her photograph: her daughters, in full rain gear, soaking wet, wearing crowns of flowers to celebrate spring. She took a video of her class's dance around the maypole with ribbons. Of course parents still came. No one wanted to disappoint their children, maybe especially now.

The next day was Mother's Day. She had slept in, just thirty minutes, when she heard a fall in the next room. The toddler had fallen off her high chair, trying to climb across the table to get the remnants of her sister's chocolate Easter bunny, and had a goose egg and a black eye. They would have to spend the entire day watching her, to see if they would have to go to urgent care. At one point the mother left for the farmers' market by herself, to pick up flowers for the nature table. Closed tulips with the promise of yellow. Another teary, necessary solo walk. They were supposed to see the cherry blossoms in full bloom, but they canceled. The storm would take them down anyway.

All that spring and summer, the children are sick again—fevers, runny noses, sore throats. Will this meditation end, she wonders, with the children, with all of them, finally getting the virus that for two years they've rearranged their lives to forestall? The tests keep coming back negative, and there is pollen everywhere. There is also another outbreak of rats, which crawl into their elderly car and eat up the wiring in the engine bay. She is reminded of Jane Bennett's contingent tableau in *Vibrant Matter*: "a dead rat, some oak pollen, and a stick of wood." Will this meditation end, perhaps, with the toddler getting vaccinated, sometime this summer, as was promised? Will it end by the close of summer, when she is finally two, and has to wear a mask as well? Does it end? Does it end?

The Summer Book

The beauty of summer with small children, how one has no choice but to give oneself over to it. She had to start thinking again of summer clothes, as the girls had outgrown everything—their drawers were empty of colorful shorts and tanks, of baseball caps that properly fit their heads, of rash guards and water shoes, waiting with other overheated children through early heat waves for the sprinklers to be turned on at their tiny neighborhood playground. Mostly it's a new crew of toddlers, she can see, in bucket hats and baseball caps, dazed, holding plastic bubble sticks and water shooters from the dollar store, although some parents she knows are also back with second children, looking exhausted. When they run into a child from the past, even if it's only been months, they remark how much taller and older they look. Eating grapes and cheese on the bench for snack time, kept cool with ice packs. Watery foods—cucumbers, watermelon, cantaloupe. Traveling to playgrounds, sometimes for swings, for better splash pads. Pushing endless swings. Her daughter trying to master the monkey bars.

Could this notebook be titled instead "Iridescences"? Soap bubbles, slicked limbs, gasoline sheen, butterfly wings, neon pieces of popped water balloons.

The palette for their simple spring and summer clothes, meant to be changed a million times a day, is now yellows and peaches, some pinks and purples. The girls insist on dressing alike, which surprises her—they beg for the same jackets, the same color shorts and tees. They beg for tees with graphic prints, like strawberries or dogs, which are more expensive. Almost every day a bag of laundry to sort, to hang up to dry, to fold. The summer laundry can't be done fast enough. Chocolate ice cream, sunscreen, caked with dirt. If she were to write a memoir now, she would call it *The Melancholy of Laundry*.

As last summer wore on, she remembers, and the heat waves became more intense, the mother had started to feel claustrophobic and miserable with the grayness and the heat. Not taking the baby out during the heat meant not going outside herself. Spooky heat—a flash of the future for her children, which they are living now. That June, the babysitter—a former grad student who comes a couple times a week during the baby's naps in the early summer, to take their older daughter to the park, before they decide to put her in summer camp—made a comment during a particularly strenuous heat wave in the Pacific Northwest. Why have children, she said in front of the daughter, we'll all be dead in fifteen years. The callousness of such nihilism and despair. When there are real consequences for children now.

A report of the collapse of insect populations, the beginning of the sixth mass extinction. A day last summer when she needed to seek out the butterflies in the forest, the family goes together to Lookout Hill in Prospect Park. Red Admirals, Nabokov's butterflies of doom. The white cabbage butterflies. The dog-day cicadas. The bark, everywhere in the park, peeling off the trees.

Last summer they returned to the Nethermead for the summer session of the forest school—only the two older friends are left, along with several new younger children. The children still told to wear masks, despite the heat. Still, a pleasure, almost

KATE ZAMBRENO

nostalgic, to go back—to the same field since the baby was a newborn, to the commons at Prospect Park, to the same linden tree, so tall that it looks like it's been reshaped many times—to gather on plastic blankets, to sing songs in Spanish. They visit three great trees near the boathouse, where the three trails intersect. She takes pictures of her girls in the deep hollow of the tree, with its blue-gray sinewy limbs.

In that summer of newborn babies, they are in session with a couple who are both moral philosophers (she learned by searching their names later), the woman nine months pregnant, ready to give birth. Online she reads an essay they cowrote on sharing childcare, about what they call the "daddy dividend," meaning that even when a heterosexual couple thinks that they are sharing childcare, the fathers get to do the activities that are more high-profile, more fun—in contrast with the constant invisible reproductive labor and mental load of the mother. Although she knows that her partner wants to be there in the muck of the home and the family, try as they might, their roles aren't the same. She is amused by the moral philosophers at the parent-child forest school, and it becomes a recurring private joke between her and her partner. All these couples at the forest school, the fathers talking to one another, the mothers watching the children. She feels irritated by many dads there, as well as at her daughter's kindergarten the next year, the painters who stand around at drop-off and talk with her partner about art, before going to their studios for hours and hours, while their wives are at home taking care of younger children, doing housework. She is resentful because she doesn't have such time herself, doesn't have space, or a studio, barely has time to prep for school. No restoration, all care work and maintenance labor. But that's the way one creates art, her partner says. Time. He gets no such time either. But isn't there a way, she asks him, to argue for art that is about taking care of others? She wonders if that is partially what she's writing about: that there's art, or at least a contemplative life, to be found in care work. That there can be great meaning in such labor, which is undervalued and underrecognized. He agrees, which feels like a distance has been crossed over the past two years.

There are seashells around the linden tree. Always a gentle mystery as to who left them. The children paint the shells with mud. The ecstasy, when one is able to see it, of watching children play with mud. On another Tuesday, she takes a photograph of the tiniest spiderweb at the root of the linden tree, which has trapped the tiniest blue moth. She then shows the web to the children.

Sometime that July, trying to write a little bit of her winter notebook every day, feeling vertiginous writing in a different season, most of the time on the couch, breastfeeding the baby, she writes to her friend Sofia about all this, about the ecstasy of being at the foot of the linden tree with children. Their older daughter's drop-off summer camp allows the mother to have two hours of nap time, with the baby on top of her, sometimes one more hour of work if she takes a second nap. How both partners jealously guard this nap time; it's the only time they have to get any thinking done.

Her daughter is happy going to summer camp at the park, being part of a group, in matching red tees, lounging around on plastic tarps, singing songs. Very loose themes. During "art week" they color a piece of paper blue, which could possibly be a boat. Just before "nature week," though, they receive a message that lice have been found in the school. Perhaps that counts, she joked to her partner. They often go to the park together for pickup. The goal, she writes to Sofia, is to have days when she doesn't just meld into the couch when she hasn't gotten writing done. When her daughter is home, she feels the need to be present with her, to be present with her daughter's needs—so she is, playing word games and painting toilet-roll sculptures and reading the entirety of *The Wonderful Wizard of Oz*. She finds herself sometimes even thinking longingly of the year at home, the fragile beauty of it. How long can this go on? she writes to Sofia, who has teenagers at home.

Sometime that first pandemic winter, she read in a profile that Silvia Federici, theorist of invisible domestic labor, walks every day in Prospect Park. All these past two years, she has fantasized about running into Silvia Federici. She has wondered whether perhaps she has seen her, walking in the park, in those early days. What would she ask her? Something about what to do with the constancy of reproductive labor. How to deal with the exhaustion of it. How not to have it bleed over into resentment. How to continue in tenderness and care. Her friend mentions something she remembers Federici saying in an interview: that one reason for our sad depressed politics is that we exaggerate the importance of what we can do alone. But what is the nuclear family, her friend writes, what is middle-class motherhood in this country, other than constantly exaggerating the importance of what you can do alone?

As she is standing around with the parents, watching her daughter climb the linden tree, she thinks of the history of progressive education, its socialist roots, and how, when imported into the United States, it became instead about segregation and grotesque private-school inequities. Like Reggio Emilia, that program started in Italy after World War II by working parents who wished to have a different, more collective form of childcare. She thinks of the photos of the children outside of the Casa dei Bambini, with their smocks, stacking blocks, working at their projects on tables. Of Maria Montessori, who created the Children's House in order for impoverished mothers of the San Lorenzo district to be able to go to work, and for their children to be able to learn in light-filled, hygienic, beautiful environments. A longing realized. What if it could always feel and be like this?

She wonders whether her own longing toward progressive education, of finding joy in childhood education, would always be disappointed, something like wearing the green glasses in Emerald City. A chasing of the good life, after Lauren Berlant, whose *Cruel Optimism* she read all that summer, after learning that they died. Why this model that Mark Fisher calls "capitalist realism," in which these progressive philosophies, the Montessori and Reggio Emilia and Waldorf methods first developed for the children of poor and working families—like Steiner's preschool for children of workers at the Waldorf-Astoria cigarette factory—are only widely available today in expensive private settings. For why should one have to pay so much for it? Why shouldn't all children, all parents, have access to it?

There isn't a parent she's had a conversation with, in these two years, who hasn't longed for something different, some different model of education. Such programs, like their forest school in the park, where the children work on playing together and collaboration, guided by watchful parents and a caring facilitator, took shape as parent cooperatives in the wake of fascism. These years, in the commons, in the space where parents have had to invent pods and cooperatives in order to help one another, in order to keep working, for they were always expected to keep working, she has wondered about who gets what type of education and who does not. She thinks of the sacrifices she's made for her daughter's education, how all of it was labor, even though so much of it is also love, and of how often she is made to feel it isn't real work at all, even though it is.

Some afternoons after summer camp, a ritual that will repeat the following summer, they take both daughters to the massive splash pad, a large, level basin that in the winter is the park's ice-skating rink, with fountains spraying at the edges. She watches her older daughter run around and around in circles, and then, the first summer, and then more the next, her sister begins to chase after her. She watches the teem of children run around splashing in chest-deep water, the absolute glee of their din. She is reminded of that moment in *Territory of Light*, a summer of dazed heat, when the mother gets in trouble with the landlord for not noticing that the rooftop has flooded, as that was her responsibility, one of the reasons her rent was discounted. But when she and her daughter are led to the terrace, they are dazzled by the sparkling water, as if they've discovered the sea, and they run about, splashing each other. The misery of the landlord and their lives, the ecstasy when the mother and daughter can be together.

How invisible children have been these two years, because they are seen as outside of capitalism. How better possibilities must exist, for a future for children.

Last August, her daughter had begged to go back to their family cabin. They will go again, inevitably, this summer, and they are making plans for it. Last summer, they had been reluctant to make the three-day drive through the Midwest, with a small baby who despised the car and wanted to nurse constantly. Why can't I ever be a country mouse? her daughter had cried. Her friends scattered to grandparents' homes along the Eastern Seaboard, in places like Cape Cod, or to houses upstate, or increasingly to rented houses in France. The mother wanted to give a respite in nature to her daughter. To give her the summers she herself had as a child. Some sense as well of her ancestry. So finally they got up in the middle of the night and started driving, through heavy storms that paralyzed highways, from a hurricane that never made landfall but made torrents of rain, until they were deep into the hills of Pennsylvania nearing dawn.

After they arrived and settled in, her father took his granddaughter for walks in the forest, looking up flowers and birds in his books, while the baby napped. Something like the solitude of the grandmother and daughter in Tove Jansson's *The Summer Book*, which she was reading. The cabin is where her father was most his essential self, was most in touch with being a child. And so was she as well, able to remember being a child, being a daughter. She thought of the mythical portrait of her father and uncle, the twins, dressed identically in short overalls and striped shirts, probably the age of her oldest now, while up at camp. And of the other framed photo, the one that hangs in the largest bedroom at the cabin, of the two boys, somewhat older, playing basketball. Their father, her grandfather, took those photographs, and printed them himself in photogravure, in his darkroom off the kitchen at the Oak Park house. Perhaps this summer she will learn to use her grandfather's camera, which sits still and heavy in a shopping bag.

The trees that once were so short, behind the basketball hoop, are now full-grown. The lives of these trees, now seventy to eighty years old. She thinks of the time, on a visit to her father's house three summers ago, when she watched a film her aunt had had transferred to DVD, of children bobbing and laughing in the waters up at the cabin, before the dock was even built. She didn't know, then, why they wanted her to watch it. Almost everyone in the film was either elderly, now, or dead. It sometimes feels like all she has heard from her father and her aunt, in the past two years, is which of the children in that video have now died. She found it intensely morbid then, almost ghoulish, like Roland Barthes's sentimental fixation on his mother as a child. *Camera Lucida*, the French title not quite translatable, an inversion of the term for the darkroom where a photograph was developed. But wasn't that also on the lock screen of her phone—her own photo, the curly heads of two little girls from last summer, in matching denim dungarees, near the water, poking their sticks in the mud? They remind her so much of her and her sister, one dark and one fair. Wasn't this what she was always thinking about? That that moment didn't exist anymore? That it exists only in the impossible space of that photograph—in that room of light.

ACKNOWLEDGMENTS

This collection of meditations could not have been written without the community of parents and teachers I spent time with, mostly in Prospect Park, during those first years of the pandemic. Especially Paulina Trevino-Oliva and Melina Gac-Levin of Nido Forest School, as well as Rachael Zur and Anamarie Pasdar, who helped keep me sane during insane times. I also want to thank my friends—Sofia Samatar, Bhanu Kapil, Danielle Dutton, and Suzanne Scanlon especially—for being my listeners and readers even when far away, and for the example of their own work. Such gratitude to Jenny Odell, Rivka Galchen, Sabrina Orah Mark, Sinéad Gleeson, and Samantha Hunt for their early support of this book, and their own works of attention and care. To Annie Ernaux for your words, and to Alison L. Strayer for translating them at such short notice. To the John Simon Guggenheim Memorial Foundation, for the fellowship that came at a critical time. To my students, who have often taught me just as much, especially my On Time seminar at Columbia University in Fall 2020, as well as my After Nature classes at Sarah Lawrence College in 2020–2021 and 2021–2022, and my lecture on The Animal at Sarah Lawrence College in 2021–2022. Thank you to Amy Hollywood and everyone else at Harvard's Center for the Study of World Religions, for inviting me to give a talk on David Wojnarowicz's grief journal in February 2020 that would, one year later, become the research for "The Hall of Ocean Life." To the NYU Creative Writing Program, for inviting me to give a talk that would become "The Wind Was Full of Spring." To Molly Taylor at Kasmin Gallery, for inviting me to write on the work of James Rosenquist. To Harriet Moore and Cal Morgan, for championing this book into the world. To Claire Fallon, for her swift and expert fact-checks. To everyone else at Riverhead who has continued to support my books there—especially Glory Plata, Catalina Trigo, Laura Perciasepe, Susan VanHecke, Christina Caruccio, Candy Gianetti, and Ryan Boyle. I want to acknowledge especially the collaborative spirit and brilliance of Lucia Bernard, the interior designer who helped me realize my visions with the look and feel of *Drifts* and *The Light Room*. To John Vincler, my partner, co-parent, and collaborator—it would all be impossible without you. And to Leo and Rainer—my great loves and guides.